WALK INTO THE LIGHT

The Journey of a Lightworker duo

Michael & Sarah Feeley

Published by Sazmick Books

Email: walkintothelight@live.co.uk
Web: http://www.walkintothelight.co.uk

Printed in Great Britain by www.direct-pod.com
Brixworth, Northampton.

DEDICATIONS:

This book is dedicated to each other and to the light workers out there who strive to make the world a better place and who assist in the ascension of humanity. Keep fighting the good fight!

Also dedicated to the memory of Sarah Jenson

(1836 – 1850)

Our spiritual sister!

ACKNOWLEDGEMENTS

A big Thank you goes out to everyone mentioned in this book all of whom have given their expressed permission to be named and their involvement disclosed. All are real people spreading the message of 'Love & Light' and without them many of these events could not have been told.

Our expressed gratitude goes to our friends and our inspiration:

Sue Orchard (Cottage Healing Centre, Tamworth): For your guidance and your teachings during our continued journey of light.

Richard Keogh (Angelman): For your teachings and friendship during our journey and of course for all of your jokes!

Sarah Jenson (Now in spirit): Although in spirit thank you for being with us and guiding us towards our purpose.

Karen (Clairvoyant): For your assistance in the initial period of our need when we turned to you for help.

Thank you to our friends at the cottage healing centre who are too numerous to mention individually, for your energy and companionship.

Thank you to Ascended Masters Saint Germain and Paul the Venetian for your spiritual influence and guidance during the writing of this book, for allowing our artistic expression to flourish.

Thank you to Archangel Gabriel "Messenger of God" for your influence and guidance during this project, for allowing the truth to manifest into the written word with such ease.

Our Family:

Thank you to Kate (Sarah's Mother),

Thank you to Charlotte (Sarah's sister): For both being there for us and offering your support during a difficult and needy time in our lives.

Thank you to Ann and John (Mick's Mom and Stepdad): For taking us in when we needed to be around others.

And last but not least, all members of our family whether or not mentioned in this book, for your continual Love and support.

It is said that before we are born into the physical world we choose our parents. We made a good choice... You are our polarity and our strength.

'IN LOVE & THANKS TO YOU ALL'

NAMASTE!
("I bow to the divine in you")

CONTENTS

Acknowledgements   v

About The Authors   ix

Chapter 1: Genesis, The Start Of A Journey   1

Chapter 2: Sarah Jenson. What Really Happened.   9

Chapter 3: Healing   21

Chapter 4: Angels, Guides & Ascended Masters   27

Chapter 5: Celestial Visitation   39

CHAPTER 6: An out of body experience & the Cottage stay over   51

CHAPTER 7: Close encounters   59

CHAPTER 8: Galactic Federation of Light   75

CHAPTER 9: Crop Circles   81

CHAPTER 10: Michael's meditations   87

CHAPTER 11: Sarah's meditations   93

CHAPTER 12: Conclusion   101

About The Authors

Michael & Sarah Feeley met in 2006 and after a short time together they married in August 2008.

Now as husband and wife their spiritual path has become one that is accelerated and events have unfolded at a breath taking pace which has astonished not only themselves but also others around them. They had always been open minded to many things but hadn't really taken any action in relation to spirituality.

Both Michael and Sarah decided to put their careers in the police force on hold in order to 'walk into the light'. Between them they served for 21 years. Many of the sightings and events covered in Chapter 7 occurred when they were on duty, giving the events even more credence.

They both realised that happiness and freedom transcends everything else and that their 'Divine path and mission' which they are fortunate enough to be walking together, is where their life belongs in the service of others spreading the love and light of the Divine Oneness.

In early 2009 all changed with a bump in the night. Since then they have been visited by Angels and Archangels, Ascended Masters and Spirit guides on a regular basis and have a cosmic being named Amanda, guiding them. This book will cover all of their experiences over a period of time in which their spiritual growth has taken an accelerated path with true cosmic guidance.

Their story will amaze you and change your life forever and will give you, the reader reassurance that death is not the end. Our physical bodies may die but our Soul is infinite...

Neither Mick nor Sarah were spiritual people until the events of 2008 and 2009 occurred. Now they are ready to share their experiences with others in the hope that it will inspire and enlighten them and jog the memories of their souls.

In this book the subjects are dealt with in depth, however there are some topic areas that are only touched upon and it would be beneficial for the reader to conduct their own research into these subjects, the information of which is readily available.

Sarah and I are 'Twin Flames or Twin Souls' who have come to Earth at this time for a Divine purpose. We don't fully understand or know that exact purpose yet but there is a reason we are here. We have had many lifetimes together one being in Atlantis and we have joined forces in service once again in these times, Earth is going through a change in Energy as we get ever nearer to 2012 when ascension will take place for many who are ready and have lifted their vibrations sufficiently.

Humankind is currently residing in the third dimension and we are aiming to reach the fifth dimension in line with our cosmic families and other beings who have already reached these heights.

We all have twin flames but both will not necessarily incarnate on the Earth together. Usually one will incarnate and one will act as a guide for the incarnated soul but it is possible that both will come together if there is a particular mission of importance or it is to be the last Earthly lifetime. They may just work together for a Divine purpose.

Sarah and I are very fortunate in the fact that we are not only twin flames or twin souls with a Divine purpose but we have also been given the fantastic opportunity to have a physical relationship on this Earth plane which isn't necessarily always the case. We are very grateful that this gift has been afforded to us so that we can enjoy not only the spiritual but also the physical together. We have the best of everything, and thanks can only be given for that.

So without further adieu, Michael and Sarah would like to take you on their journey of discovery and ask you to walk into the light.

Read their story, the journey of a Lightworker duo...

CHAPTER 1: GENESIS, THE START OF A JOURNEY

In the 1800's the Kingstanding area of Birmingham in the UK was farmland and unlike today these times saw village life and smaller communities.

Serious matters could be disguised without question and crimes could go un-investigated and passed off easily without argument, there was no such thing as forensic evidence.

In these times a young 14 year old girl by the name of Sarah Jenson lived in this area with her Mother and Step- Father. It is unknown whether or not the family extended further than that but it is easy to imagine that it did due to the size of the family units in those times.

One night in around 1850 Sarah Jenson mysteriously died and her death was passed off as an illness and no questions were asked. It was not unusual for this to happen. Nothing else was said or done in relation to the mystery death of the 14 year old Victorian teenager.

Over One Hundred years later Kingstanding looked completely different being an urban town and part of a large city but nevertheless energy from vanished times still remained despite the surge of brick and mortar and the birth of the modern day. The area still held secrets and stories that had remained untold despite being buried by progress and the modern age.

Shortly after 1983 when my Wife and co-author Sarah was born, her and her family moved into a house in Kingstanding which was built, as were all the other houses, on top of what used to be farmland. This is where Sarah Jenson would have lived with her family.

Sarah's family lived in the house for generations and it saw Sarah, her older sister Charlotte and her younger brother Kevin growing up. Nothing at the time could have given any clues or indication as to the history that lay beneath them and right under their feet.

The family only became aware of Sarah Jenson one morning in 1993 when Sarah and her brother Kevin were lying in their Mother's bed waiting for their breakfast. Sarah was ten years of age at the time and Kevin three.

Sarah describes this event from here on:

"On this particular morning, Kevin and I were lying there awake waiting for our Mom Kate, who was making us breakfast in bed. As we lay there Kevin began to giggle at me and said "You look like Sarah Jenson". I immediately thought this was a strange thing for my three year old brother to say as he was only just getting used to using people's first names. I asked Kevin who Sarah Jenson was and he cheekily covered his face and continued to giggle as if he had done something naughty. Kevin would frequently laugh when he was giving one of us the run around! I asked him if Sarah Jenson was a friend from the street and still laughing he replied "No". I asked if she was a friend from nursery and he said "No". He kept glancing over to the end of the bed near to the mirror on our Mom's wardrobe. I asked again who Sarah Jenson was and Kevin quickly pointed over towards the wardrobe at the end of the bed and said "There she is". This was getting really strange and just then our Mom walked into the bedroom with our breakfast.

I began to tell her what Kevin had been saying and she too thought this was somewhat strange. She questioned Kevin asking the same questions and Kevin kept replying "There she is" or "She's over there now". Mom would walk towards wherever Kevin pointed and each time it seemed Sarah Jenson would move. Kevin said "She's moved now cause you stood by her, she's in the mirror now". To Kevin it didn't seem that anything odd was taking place. He could see this girl and found the whole thing amusing because neither my Mother nor I could see her. It was like they were playing some kind of game with us.

Moms' face was white and she could hardly believe the things her three year old son was saying, but she knew it was the truth.

There had been strange stories about the house we lived in for many years. It was classed as the haunted house of the street. Weird things did happen there over the years, some quite scary but I guess you just get used to it after a time. It was home and that to us was what our particular home was like. It was a part of our family history and upbringing. I have the upmost respect for our Mother because she refused to let these things bother her or any of us. She would walk around the house with her holy water and tell the noisy spirits where to go! With respect though. It seemed to work for a short time but the events would always persist soon after.

Kevin was not the only person to see Sarah Jenson and it seemed she loved it whenever children were around. It was a chance to have fun and play with them. This was evident when some years later my young cousin Jamie came to visit with his mother. Jamie was also around three or four at the time and whenever he came to visit he would run straight up to Kevin's bedroom to play. Kev's room was like kiddie Heaven, filled with toys, cars, wrestling rings and action men. Kids that visited seemed to disappear for hours into the unknown!

He had been up there for quite some time when he suddenly appeared in the living room. He was laughing quietly but nervously and said to my Mom Kate, "Kate, I don't want to play with the girl upstairs anymore, I've been playing for ages but she wants me to carry on playing with her".

Our faces hit the floor. Kevin was out at school, I'd had the day off and there was no one else in the house except our Mothers. Bewildered my Mom calmly said to Jamie "It's ok Jamie, you don't have to play with her if you don't want to, you can stay down here now if you like", trying not to alarm him in any way. Jamie's Mom was aware of the Sarah Jenson story but this was the only first hand experience she had had with us.

Eventually my Mom made some enquiries into the history of the house and decided to see if she could uncover anything about Sarah Jenson. To our amazement, she did find something. She had managed to speak with a really old couple that used to live facing our house. It turned out they remembered hearing something about a Jenson family that lived within our vicinity, but this was before their time. They had heard about the families' young girl, who they were confident, was named Sarah that had died mysteriously. She was only around thirteen or fourteen years old at the time and the story was that she had lost her sight due to voiles disease caused by rats in the area, and died.

Nothing more was ever done but now we knew for definite that the little girl my brother Kevin and Cousin Jamie saw was not make believe, although we knew that anyway. After all, how could a three year old just come up with a name he had never heard before, whom just happened to have lived in that area before he was born?

Eventually at the age of eighteen I left home in Kingstanding followed by the rest of the family a few short years later but ever since these events I'd always had the feeling that something just wasn't quite right about the story of Sarah Jenson's death. It just didn't seem to add up. Why was this innocent young girl still hanging around and why did she love so much the company of children? I had told so many people of these occurrences in the following years and always, always felt there was more to it. I even joked with some that I had a feeling she was probably buried under the stairs and she was waiting for someone to find her. However, I wasn't to hear Sarah Jenson's name again until some years later.

In September 2004, following some very unusual experiences whilst living at my Dad's house I started to think about going to see a psychic medium. This was following an incident where a ghost walked into my room one day whilst I was in bed having been on a night shift the night before. I was unable to move and there was no one else in the house at the time as my Dad and Stepmom were both out at work. This spirit seemed more curious than anything, walking around the bed and then peering right into my face before leaving again. Through the door I hasten to add!

It didn't stop there. A few nights later I had had an early night ready for the early shift the next morning. I had been asleep about an hour when I suddenly woke up paralysed once again. The only thing this time was that the bed was rocking around frantically as if in the middle of an

Earthquake. All the time there was a male voice talking calmly but firmly to me from above and to my right. I was so panicked at the time that I wasn't interested in what the voice was saying. I was more concerned that my bed was being thrown around with me on it! Was I being abducted I wondered? I had seen a few UFO's in my time and read stories about people being taken. Suddenly it all began to calm down and as my bed came to rest gently back on the ground the voice said before fading away, "Save yourself". Save myself? What from I wondered? Was the shelf about to fall on my head? It looked pretty stable to me! I couldn't work out what this voice was referring to. Oddly, even though the bed had just been thrown around on the spot I was able to remain calm and collected and went straight back to sleep, now able to move again freely. I knew that I was fully conscious at the time of this incident and that whatever took place must have happened on another dimension somewhere as no-one rushed to my aid when the bed was being jolted about. But then it was at a time that 'Big Brother' was on the television!

Some days later I was introduced to my Stepmom's cousin Tina who practised Reiki, an ancient Universal energy healing, (Reiki is covered more in another chapter). She helped clear my body using this universal energy and also the room at my Dad's where I had been sleeping. She even described the spirit of an elderly lady that was with me at the time as a guide. The lady described was my Nan, also named Sarah whom had passed away before I was born. This was all becoming more and more intriguing. Tina recommended a psychic medium to me named Karen that I could see if I was still interested.

After a period of around six months living at my Dad and Stepmom's house I moved into a new place that I rented with two friends where we lived for eighteen months. It was from here that I planned a two week trip to Goa with another friend and her family set for January 2006. It was also shortly after this trip that Mick and I began seeing each other.

Before going to Goa I finally decided to book that appointment with Karen the medium. I spoke with her on the phone and booked my appointment for the day after I arrived back from Goa. All she needed was for me to provide my first name and to turn up on the day. I definitely felt like I needed to go see a medium. I was curious to know what was going on around me as I seemed to have grown up with all these strange experiences.

When I returned I was excited about my appointment with Karen but also a little dubious as to what she may or may not tell me. I attended my appointment and began having my reading in the kitchen. The whole appointment lasted around thirty minutes but during it Karen kept referring to a spirit coming through for me by the name of Sarah Johnson, or similar. This spirit was the first to come through and Karen emphasized that she was insistent that she was for me. For some reason, the name Sarah Johnson didn't ring any bells for me and each time this spirit popped up I confirmed that the name meant nothing to me.

The rest of the information divulged during the reading was accurate and certainly gave me a lot to think about. In fact, I was amazed at how accurate the reading was and couldn't wait to tell family and friends of the contact I had had with relatives passed on. My Granddad David and my Uncle Paddy were amongst those that made an appearance so to speak. However I was still left wondering who Sarah Johnson was. I was still none the wiser but this had stirred up my interest.

It bugged me for several weeks until I eventually had a eureka moment, long overdue I know! I realised that Karen must have meant Sarah Jenson. I was aware that sometimes information can be distorted as it is passed to the channeller from spirit and messages aren't always that clear. This brought the Sarah Jenson story back to the forefront of my mind and I asked myself why she would try and make contact with me. I kicked myself that I hadn't realised during the reading that this was who was trying to get through to me. I somehow felt connected to Sarah and knew that she must have been trying to tell me something important.

I told Mick about the story of Sarah Jenson and explained my feelings about the whole thing. I knew there was more to this than meets the eye.

I didn't know what to do and so again the mystery of Sarah Jenson was left unheard for a couple more years. But next time it resurfaced, it wasn't going away".

Sarah and I had always as individuals been interested in ghosts, UFO's and alike and although Sarah had had several experiences of a paranormal kind, I had not yet seen anything to date. It wasn't until shortly after we began our relationship that we actually started to experience these kind of phenomenal occurrences together.

In July 2006 we moved into a house together which was to be our new family home. We worked together sharing the same days off and life was great, except for one little thing... our health. Our health seemed to be deteriorating and both Sarah and I always seemed to be ill with constant headaches, back pain, feeling drained of energy and forever catching a cold. Our moods began to change and we seemed to be downhearted and ill tempered. This was especially true of me. We put this down to working on shifts and doing long hours and never really allowing our bodies the chance to get into a comfortable routine. Sarah remembers feeling drained of energy for quite a number of years and so had gotten used to the lack of energy but this was new to me. However, it wasn't long before I too became used to feeling this way.

This didn't stop our love for each other though and in August of 2008 Sarah and I married. So far this was one of the most memorable days of our life, not only because the planning, preparation and day itself ran beautifully, but because there were no family bust ups of any kind. This in itself is strange for Sarah's family! We knew then we and the marriage were definitely meant to be. We went away on our honeymoon which also ran smoothly, returning two weeks later. This was the turning point.

In the few weeks leading up to the wedding we had a sudden interest in alternative view points and conspiracies and information seemed to be falling at our feet. We learned to look at the world in a different way and not to always take things at face value. This information continued to reveal itself to us and was here that our journey began. I would say that this is where our great awakening began, with the information provided transitioning nicely from one topic to the next. It was from this point that we had opened ourselves up and shared many weird and wonderful experiences together.

A couple of months later in October Sarah and I were at home and sat side by side on the sofa. We were on the internet looking at various things of interest to us at the time when all of sudden we heard the loudest crack of glass. We had momentarily ducked our heads as we realised that someone must have thrown a brick at our double glazed French window. We looked to our right where this window is situated and saw that the six foot pane of glass was shattered from top to bottom. Realising that if we were quick enough we might catch the culprits responsible running off, we immediately put our shoes on and darted outside within a matter of seconds. "If I get hold of the little so and so's" I thought to myself.

It suddenly dawned on us that there wasn't a soul around and the sounds we thought we might hear of scurrying teenagers, could not be heard. We walked back to our garden and over to the shattered window at the side of the house. We expected to see a stone or brick lying near by but there was nothing to be seen. We only had a very small patioed garden so rebounding stones and bricks wouldn't be able to travel very far. As we got closer to the window we could see the point of impact in the middle of the pane where the glass had shattered outwards. The only thing was, to our amazement, there wasn't even a scratch on the outer pane of glass. The window had shattered from the inside.

This was weird. We both returned inside the house and saw that the window had indeed shattered from within. How could this happen? There was nothing by it that could have accidently landed on it. It was a fairly new window and wasn't under any pressure. And it was a normal day, no extreme weather conditions or anything of the kind. So how did this happen?

For some unknown reason myself and Sarah suddenly burst into fits of laughter! We found the whole incident hysterical! We put it down to some kind of energy bolt maybe one of us had sent out somehow. We knew that everything that exists is made up of energy and so maybe that was it. It remained a mystery for a short while.

Following this various other occurrences took place including the time when the hands on my manual watch had been put back by exactly one hour, but the date remaining unaltered. Events seemed to be increasing and looking back it now seems they were building up towards something much bigger.

It was now nearing Christmas and both Sarah and I had learned more about the world in general and the illusion a lot of us live under. Sarah had a calling to learn Reiki and had organised this for the following weeks, and both of us had an urge to have a psychic reading. The medium Sarah had seen in 2006 was the likely candidate and so we booked our appointment for two days before Christmas. For me this urge was more out of curiosity and I had never done anything like this before. With the day booked I was quietly looking forward to the event.

The day soon arrived and we had our readings separately. I went in first not knowing what to expect, a little apprehensive. Karen was quick to put me at ease and assured me there was nothing to feel nervous about. The reading quickly got under way and I was delighted that many family members that were on the other side came through to speak to me and to give me their messages of love and encouragement. It seemed they were very proud of me and this in turn made me feel equally proud. The whole event was recorded on tape.

During the reading Karen asked me if I was always feeling drained, sleeping well but waking up tired with lower back pain and feeling generally under the weather. I told her this was correct and I had been feeling that way for some time. She then proceeded to tell me that I had a negative energy around me and in our house which was feeding off of my own energy. This was what was making me feel the way I had been feeling. I hadn't really any understanding of what this meant and thought that this negativity was probably my own attitude at that time. Karen gave me some ways of dealing with this suggesting the use of sea salts around the house and a glass of water on the window sill.

My thirty minutes was up and I was very impressed with my time. It was now Sarah's turn. I left the house and waited outside leaving Sarah to have her reading. She describes here how that reading went:

"Well I went in and having met Karen at my first reading a couple of years earlier, felt instantly comfortable. I wasn't sure she would remember me but she did. I listened as she began describing current events in my life and likely events that could be avoided. Not so many of my family members came through for me this time but a number of Mick's family, whom I had never had the privilege of meeting before, did. This was an honour and they wanted to inform me that they were thankful to me and that they were very proud of Mick and I. Karen then went on to describe a negative energy around me and in our house. Sound familiar? Incidentally this is what she had told me two years previous when I had seen her and I didn't really understand it then either. Like Mick I assumed it was because I was unhappy at work and thought it was my attitude generally. My housemate had also been to see Karen some time after me a couple of years ago and she too was told about a negative energy surrounding her at home. This was when we lived in our rented accommodation together.

Anyway, I digress! Karen explained to me that this had come up in Mick's reading also and had told him how we could help deal with it, but she seemed unsure of the cause. The reading went on and at the end she asked me if I had any questions that I would like to ask. I had already planned a question but that changed at the last moment and what I said to Karen was "You mentioned a girl named Sarah Johnson two years ago. I didn't understand it then but I do now. Is she still around"? I explained that the name was in fact Jenson and not Johnson. Karen paused for a moment closing her eyes and then a wry smile entered her face. "Oh yes, she's still around" she said "And she likes you. In fact she has attached herself to you. She looks a lot like you", just as Kevin had said years ago. I didn't understand what a spirit attachment was at the time so I asked. Karen explained that spirits that stay on the Earth plane instead of crossing over when they have died often attach themselves to someone or something as a source of energy to keep going. This has the same affect as on a battery and they will wear down the energy of the being they are attached to as they are literally stealing that person's energy. Karen explained that this was the negative energy she had talked about surrounding us.

Sarah wanted to tell me that there was more to her death than appeared on the surface and that she wanted me to look into it. Karen stated that she was feeling that Sarah Jenson had been taken by 'another's hand' and that she could send her away now if I wished. It was confirmed that we were talking about a possible murder. I told Karen that I had always felt that there was something more behind the story of Sarah Jenson. I decided to help Sarah and explained I would see what I could do. Sarah was saying that I would easily find her. The medium stated that if I needed any help with Sarah at any time then to just call. She could help her to pass safely over to the other side. So that was it. I was now aware of what had been causing me and the energy of others to feel so worn down.

I thanked Karen for her time and went on my way, Mick and I explaining the events of each others readings on our way home. I also immediately informed my Mom of the outcome as I knew she would be intrigued to know"!

From then on we could feel Sarah Jenson's presence around us and a few strange things happened including on Christmas day whilst opening presents when a photograph of me and Sarah fell for no reason whatsoever from the corner of a mirror in the living room and face down onto the floor. It was almost as if a little reminder from Sarah Jenson that she was still around waiting patiently or impatiently, we didn't know which, for Sarah to fulfil her promise.

CHAPTER 2: SARAH JENSON. WHAT REALLY HAPPENED.

During the coming weeks myself and Sarah spent hours at Birmingham library checking every death recorded in the UK from 1960 to the current year of 2009 under the name Jenson and similar. We didn't have any exact date and tried to work out when the Jenson family could possibly have lived at Sarah's old house on Twickenham Road thinking that maybe they could have been two or three generations before her own family.

Unfortunately we were unable to find anything and although disappointed, we couldn't think of any other way to uncover what we needed to know. We did consider speaking to the police but at that point it was going to be difficult, I mean what would we say? That a spirit had asked us to look into her death?! We wanted to at least have some evidence to place before them before we reported anything and at that moment, we were lacking anything other than what we knew in our hearts to be true.

As the days and weeks went by we put the matter to the back of our minds and life just got in the way. An atmosphere was definitely building and we felt as though we were being watched and waited on. A neighbour's cat that would stay with us from time to time would sit in the living room and stare intently up the staircase. She would then walk up as if being called and we would often find her lying on our bed like she was being stroked by someone. Then one day, she turned nasty and aggressive for no reason as though she was being influenced.

By now we were into the New Year and we were still no further with our quest. However if I am honest, we had given up. We couldn't see what else it was we could do.

Well on Sunday the 8th of February 2009, the situation was going to be brought to a head, whether we were ready for it or not.

 Sarah and I went out for the afternoon to a local Hotel for Sunday lunch.

Over dinner we ended up talking about Sarah Jenson and how we felt about the situation. We both agreed that we were not serving anyone by keeping her hanging in a plane of existence she didn't belong in. Besides that we didn't know what else to do. The medium had said she could help to take Sarah across to the other side where she was meant to be and we agreed that this would be the best course of action and we would take her up on her offer. We wanted to see Sarah off into the light so to speak. This was also around about the time that we had talked about starting a family. We had not mentioned this to anyone, not even our own families. We finished our lunch and returned home having decided what to do next, however things weren't right.

As soon as we walked into the house both of us could sense an eerie atmosphere and something had changed. Sarah often in the colder months would get home and stand by the living room radiator for several minutes to warm herself up. On this occasion as she rested herself against the radiator she suddenly felt the heat drain away from it and the whole thing turn cold as if it had been switched off. When she said this across the room to me, we both looked at each other in disbelief just knowing that something strange was going on. We both realised that although our intentions were that of for the good of all, we had upset Sarah Jenson with our decision to send her to the other side. There was a feeling of tension in the air and we both felt on edge in our own home. Somehow, we both knew that it wasn't going to stop there.

Sarah messed around with the heating for a while and then sat down on the sofa, taking out the laptop to browse the internet. I put on the television and sat next to her, playing around with the Tv channels. Neither of us had spoken so much as a word to each other as we both felt very nervy. Sarah began shaking her head in annoyance at the slowness that the computer was taking to load. All of a sudden I felt myself starting to turn very angry. I felt aggressive and nasty and began to snap at Sarah, not physically but verbally. I knew that this was not me and I had no idea where it had come from. Sarah looked at me rather disgraced and asked "What the hell is your problem"? She walked off upstairs quite upset and I remained seated. She returned a few minutes later and sat next to me. "What's wrong"? She asked. "I don't know" I replied. The next thing I remember was my eyes starting to feel funny. I felt dizzy and began going into tunnel vision. I went tingly all over and felt as though someone or something was trying to take over my body. I actually felt like I was being possessed. I fought as hard as I could and started resisting. I refused to give in and held on for sixty seconds or so and then the moment passed. All the while Sarah could see that something was happening to me and was trying to bring me round.

I regained my normal state of consciousness and explained to Sarah what had just happened to me. She told me she knew exactly what was happening and also knew that it wasn't me snapping at her for no reason several minutes earlier.

A possession. I had actually just fought off a possession. I remember thinking to myself that this is the kind of thing you see in movies. Not here. Not in our house. Not to us.

From that moment we made the executive decision to call Karen the medium right away. Whatever was going on, whatever Sarah Jenson was up to had to stop now. I dialled the number in desperation but to my dismay there was no reply. The call just rang out. "I'm not giving up" I thought. "I've got to keep ringing until someone answers". I dialled the number over and over again. I must have rang at least five or six times but there was just no-one answering. We sat there for five minutes evaluating what we were going to do next when our phone began to ring. To my relief it was Karen. She explained that she had been at an evening out and couldn't answer her phone before but she just felt that there was something urgent she was needed for.

I explained to Karen that we had seen her in December for a reading and that she had stated that if we ever needed her help with Sarah Jenson, that we should just give her a call. I explained exactly what was happening to us and that it was getting beyond our comfort zone. As I spoke with Karen Sarah and I had noticed that the atmosphere had once again changed only now it had returned to a normal, peaceful state. I told this to Karen who quickly replied "Yes, that's because she's now here with me giving me grief"! Karen was referring to Sarah Jenson. "She's saying you promised to help her and you haven't done anything" Karen continued. I explained that we had spent hours in Birmingham library trying to find anything remotely related to Sarah Jenson but there just wasn't a trace. What else were we to do? Karen said she was free for ten o'clock the following morning and that if we could pick her up, she would come to our home and sort out this situation. I asked her to ask Sarah Jenson if she would please give us a peaceful night. Karen said she would do her best. We made the agreement and ended the conversation.

Sarah had overheard the conversation and we were both happy to wait it out until the next morning. Surely things couldn't get any worse.

The atmosphere turned somewhat strange again as we sat in silence on the edge of our seats. Night time set in and it was now ten o'clock. We felt as though we were being watched all the time and an air of anger directed towards us. Sarah had visions of a young Sarah Jenson sat on the spiral staircase, head in her hands staring right at us. Watching... Waiting... Sarah and I the object of her frustrations. Still on the edge of our seats Sarah's head turned slowly towards me asking "Can you smell that"? Yes. I could smell it. There was an extremely strong smell of flowers wafting around us and although beautifully scented, this was enough to make us leave for the night. "Let's get out for the night" Sarah exclaimed. I completely agreed. We needed some company this night to help us to relax. Too much had happened and we needed a break! Sarah got on the phone to her Mother Kate and asked if it was okay for us to stay there on this night. Naturally this was no problem for Kate and the family. She seemed the right person to go to as she was aware of Sarah Jenson and knew that we weren't crazy!

We ran upstairs to pack our night bag but as soon as we both entered the bedroom, we were covered in goose bumps. The temperature dropped and the atmosphere was awful. I had heard accounts of this sort of thing from other people and now I realised that it was true. We threw the bare minimum into a holdall, quickly put our shoes on and left the house. We couldn't get out quick enough. We got into our car and drove to Sarah's Mom's house which was about thirty minutes away, the journey making for an interesting conversation.

As we got there we were greeted by Sarah's Mom Kate and we explained to her and Sarah's Stepdad Tony what had been occurring. We felt safer amongst other people, a sort of safety in numbers situation. We knew that the medium was coming over to help the following morning and we only needed to sit the night out.

We unpacked our things, not that we had brought a great deal with us and got into our pyjamas. We were going to be sleeping in the recently converted downstairs garage. This had been made into a lovely en suite bedroom and we were bound to have a decent night's sleep here.

We went into the living room and all watched a film until the early hours. At around one thirty in the morning we decided it was time for bed. We had had a pretty stressful day and were looking forward to the rest. We expected that everything would be fine now and that the worst was probably over. Wrong again!

We said goodnight to everyone and went to our room. Following a quick wash and the brushing of teeth, we got into bed. Strangely we left the bedside lamp on but not out of fear. This lamp gave a nice ambience and illuminated all corners of the room. This is something we never do. It was unusual that neither of us thought to switch it off or even mention it. None the less, we both lay there gazing into each others eyes and smiling in disbelief at the days events feeling somewhat more relaxed. We were both tired now and within minutes we both started to drift off to sleep.

What occurred next was to scar us for some time afterwards and neither of us were prepared for what was about to happen.

Still sleeping it was now around 03:30am on Monday the 9th of February. All of a sudden myself and Sarah woke up at the exact same time and had gone from a lying position to a sitting position. Neither of us can remember how we got there. Sarah and I have varying accounts of what happened next but this is our version of the traumatic event:

I was in this sitting position next to Sarah who was screaming hysterically. It was as though she was being viciously attacked. I was panicking and I put my hands on her to try and calm her down but nothing seemed to work. As I looked into her eyes it was like she was looking straight through me, like I was invisible. She was still screaming and unresponsive to my aid and appeared to be looking at something above my head. I gently shook her trying to get her to calm down. She was screaming "Mom, Mom". All of a sudden Sarah came round and was looking at me and started to say "What's wrong, what's wrong are you okay, you're screaming"? She had her hands on me with tears in her eyes. "I haven't been screaming" I replied "It was you, I've been trying to calm you down". Sarah continued to disagree explaining to me that it was I who had been screaming and she had been trying to calm me down but could get no response from me. She stated that she was looking at me and I had a vacant expression, like I was looking through her. She said that she had never seen a man scream so hysterically in all her life and that she was terrified. In the end she started calling for her Mom but her shouting seemed stifled and quiet. Sarah explained that as she began calling out to her Mom for help I suddenly turned to look at her as though I had just awoken from a trance. I stopped screaming and that's when I started asking her if *she* was okay.

We couldn't understand what had happened to us. Both of us were claiming that what the other was saying was what had happened to them and not the other way round. But how could such a thing occur to both of us at the same time? It was as though we had passed over briefly onto different dimensions, like time and space had been altered. That's the only thing we could think of. How else could it have happened? Both of us had awoken at the same time, started screaming hysterically in a vacant panic but neither of us can remember it. We can only remember seeing each other in this state.

I have never ever been so scared in all my life and Sarah feels the same way. Something weird had happened and it had literally scared the living daylights out of us. I've seen all of the scariest Hollywood horror movies but this was real life and we were both white with fear.

Sarah began calling to Archangel Michael as we had recently learned that he is the Angel to call in when you need help and protection. We couldn't stay in the room any longer and went and sat in the living room with every light on for comfort praying for day light when our family would wake up.

We spent the next three hours going to the toilet together and being next to each other, not letting one another out of sight. It was such relief at 7am when Kate woke up and came downstairs. Sarah was in tears and a complete wreck, completely traumatised. I was the male version of these emotions and feelings.

During breakfast Sarah's big Sister Charlotte came around to see us as she had heard about what had happened to us. She too was aware of the Jenson story. We told her what had happened to us a few hours earlier and on the now previous evening. As I began explaining to her what had happened to me at home, feeling as though I was being possessed, Charlotte began experiencing the same sensations, feeling tingly, dizzy and tunnel visioned. She went as white as a sheet and had to sit down. She sat for several minutes and then had to leave the house as she started to feel quite ill. She went on to work but was unwell all day following the visit and suffered with a bad headache.

Charlotte has since stated to us that she never really fully believed in the paranormal but now has to recognise that there may in fact be something to acknowledge.

Since we had arranged to pick up Karen the medium at 10am we left Kate's house, intent on making the twenty minute or so journey. There was myself, Sarah and Kate. Kate had wanted to come along to support us and because Sarah Jenson had been a part of her recent history too.

As we were just getting into the car Sarah received a text message to her mobile. It was from Karen the medium saying that something had come up and she couldn't make it. Instead she would give us a reading the next day. We knew that something wasn't right and out of desperation I immediately called her. We knew that this was an excuse. To my surprise she actually answered and I explained that we needed her help now! I told her everything that had happened since we last spoke the evening before and emphasized that this couldn't wait any longer. Karen agreed. My persistence had convinced her otherwise.

With that we got into Kate's car and started towards Karen's house. The tension was mounting and it felt as though we were about to commence battle.

We arrived at Karen's house to find her standing on the doorstep waiting for us. "Odd" I thought. We got out and greeted her, relieved to see each other! We all got into the car and Karen explained that during the morning there had been some strange things happening to her. Things that had made her feel uncomfortable in her own house and had put her off meeting up with us. She had been alone in the house when her coffee cup was removed from the kitchen and placed on the window sill of the living room with a spoon in it! Her washing machine had lifted off the ground and bounced around the kitchen causing it to break. She explained that it wasn't even plugged in let alone on! Karen was used to dealing with these sorts of energies but this amongst other things caused her to feel uneasy and she had not been made to feel like this in her own home before. Bearing in mind that mediums deal with all aspects of the spiritual world this is not an easy thing to do, but nevertheless it had been achieved.

It was quite clear that someone didn't want us to meet up and was doing their best to frighten all who would be involved in this cleansing.

Karen had never been to our house and didn't know where we lived so it was unusual that as we got closer to home, her stomach began to twist and hurt. As we approached our road she said "We're near".

We arrived at our house. We all built ourselves up taking some deep breaths before entering. We knew that the house wasn't the problem. It was the energy of Sarah Jenson that had attached herself to Sarah. We still felt despite all that had happened that there was something about Sarah Jenson's death that needed to surface. There was more to what was going on than just the antics of a mischievous spirit.

Sarah unlocked the door and we all went inside, the four of us arriving in the living room area. Karen had brought along her tape machine to record the event and switched it on immediately.

All of a sudden there was a noticeable temperature drop in the room and we all felt cold. Karen informed us that Sarah Jenson had just walked in. You could almost sense as this young girl strolled gently in through the doorway, obviously not needing to open it!

Although at the time invisible to all but Karen, we could all sense and feel Sarah Jenson's presence. It was difficult to comprehend at the time but we were standing in front of what many would refer to as a ghost.

Karen began to tell us that spirits like to tell their story before they move on and as well as this, Sarah Jenson was apparently having a teenage tantrum not wanting to pass to the light.

Sarah Jenson began dictating her story through Karen, explaining to us the events in her life that had lead to her death, which did in fact take place in the Kingstanding area, most likely at the land upon which Kate's families home on Twickenham Road was built. Karen first of all said "It is the anniversary of Sarah's death. That is what the flowers you could smell were for". I asked if she could give us an indication of the date we were looking at, to which Karen paused for a moment then replied "1850". That explained why we couldn't find anything at the library. The records didn't go back nearly that far.

Karen continued to allow Sarah Jenson to tell her story. "She's saying that her Stepfather used to abuse her and had abused her for quite some time. Her Mother used to stand by and let it happen" Karen stated. "On this one particular night, the night of her death her Stepfather took the abuse one step further" she continued. We knew exactly what 'one step further' meant and knew this involved the taking of Sarah Jenson's innocence. "He came into her room in the early hours of the morning, around about 3am and began the abuse. Sarah saw this coming and started to shout and scream for her Mother who never came. Her Stepfather placed his hand over her mouth and smothered Sarah to stop the screaming. Sarah struggled for breath and was suffocated. He didn't mean to kill her. He just wanted to silence her".

Karen then told us that Sarah and I had relived the experience of Sarah Jenson's death waking up at around the same time the event occurred one hundred and fifty nine years ago.

Karen proceeded to pass the messages from Sarah Jenson, telling us that her Mother and Stepfather didn't tell anyone about her death at first and tried to keep it covered up. When people realised that Sarah wasn't around anymore her Mother and Stepfather made up a story about her having died of natural causes. This is possibly where the story of voiles disease came from. Sarah Jenson continued that her body was then basically discarded without ever being given a proper burial. "I'm cold" she cried to Karen. We could see that Karen was now visibly upset herself and was feeling the emotions of Sarah Jenson. It was very upsetting for us too to listen to this poor girl's story. We felt grief stricken for her and very sorry to hear of her terrible fate.

Sarah Jenson then communicated through Karen that we only wanted to get rid of her because we had a baby on the way! As I said previously no-one knew anything about a baby other than me and Sarah and so we were shocked. It turned out that Sarah was actually pregnant but neither of us found out until months later. Slack jaw is the words I would use to describe that moment. Kate's face was also a picture as you can imagine.

At that point Karen said that we also had another spirit with us. This was the first time that this had come to light and to our astonishment it turned out to be Sarah Jenson's Stepfather who eventually gave his name as John Berkshire. He was violent and nasty and little did we realise he had been the cause of a lot of the bad feeling and ill health amongst us. It seemed he also had decided not to pass into the light as he was afraid of what was going to happen to him once he got there. He believed he would be punished for his wrong doings when he was alive and instead continued to give poor Sarah Jenson a hard time even still, whilst not in a physical embodiment. Sarah was running away from John even in the spirit world and both were feeding off our energy to continue this game of cat and mouse.

Karen explained that it was the spirit of Sarah Jenson's Stepfather John, who had been causing problems amongst ourselves and other family members. He had attempted to split Sarah and I apart and when we look back this was evident at times in some of the very sudden outbursts of anger one of us would have or an argument that ensued for no reason and out of nowhere. Apparently he wanted to cause us disruption which in turn would disrupt Sarah Jenson, preventing her from feeling safe and protected.

Karen explained that Sarah Jenson felt close to our Sarah and also felt secure being around her. This was one of the reasons she had attached herself to Sarah. Sarah Jenson had been terrified of passing over to the other side after all this time because she thought she was going back to the family that had harmed her. Karen explained to Sarah Jenson that it isn't the same on the other side and that a lot of the hurt and pain she felt was because she remained on the physical Earth plane. Karen informed us that Sarah Jenson was now shoving her arms out towards Kate, as if to push her away. To Sarah Jenson, Kate represented the Mother figure who stood by and did nothing to help her. Karen explained to Sarah that she shouldn't do that and this was not her Mother. Understandably, she wasn't particularly fond of men either as it was her own Stepfather that had caused her such pain and grief in her life.

At this point Karen was now also trying to deal with John Berkshire, who was being somewhat more difficult and abusive. Karen started to feel a choking sensation around her neck and then began receiving the story of John's death. He was also responsible for the death of someone else in his time. Who, it could not be established but on this occasion John did not get away with it. John Berkshire was hanged for murder, hence the tightening around Karen's throat. However, the murder of Sarah Jenson was never revealed, until now. It seemed that John felt intimidated by all of us and even insulted that he was being dealt with by a woman. He continued to be abusive and threatening, mainly towards the three ladies present. This kind of attitude was accepted in Victorian days but he quickly learned that this had long died out following a dressing down from Sarah's Mom Kate!

Karen then turned towards the staircase and before she had the chance to let us know of her intentions she informed us Sarah Jenson was saying to her "Ask her, you've got to ask first". Sarah Jenson was reminding Karen that she had to ask permission before she could just go upstairs. We all smiled and were humbled by Sarah Jenson's consideration and respect for ourselves and our property. Of course access to all areas was granted! We were grateful of the help.

We went to the bedroom and stood there. Karen had lit a candle, which indicated to her when John was getting close. Each time he got closer to Karen the candle flame would rise and become very tall and thin. John was being abusive to Sarah through Karen saying to her "Who do you think you are, you mind your own business". Sarah asked Karen to remind John that when his history began interfering in her life, it became her business. Karen had to pause for a second. She said she felt herself becoming very angry towards us and that this was John's anger coming out through her. She left the room to calm herself down and then returned a little more composed.

The bedroom was where Sarah Jenson spent most of her time, something that Sarah herself used to do when she lived at home in Kingstanding. Karen asked Sarah if she ever got the urge to just cut her hair off and if she often felt a shooting pain down her right arm. Surprisingly Sarah had had the urge to cut her hair off several times but fortunately never followed through! She also often would get a shooting pain up and down her right wrist and forearm. She could actually feel this at the time. Karen informed her that Sarah Jenson's Stepfather once cut a load of her hair off for no reason and that our Sarah had been picking up on this. She also said that during her attack, Sarah Jenson broke her right wrist trying to defend herself from John and this accounted for the pain Sarah now felt today.

Sarah Jenson said to Sarah the words "Thank you" and "Sorry" and felt that justice had now been done. Karen paused for a moment and informed Sarah that Sarah Jenson's favourite colours were pink and lilac. This seemed a strange thing to say at the time but it made more sense in the days to come.

Through all of this were periods of deliberate disruption including Karen's phone ringing constantly and changing ring tones of its own accord. This was John Berkshire trying to break up the event as I believe he knew he was on his way out.

Mean while , Karen informed us that she was going to step outside and lead Sarah Jenson half way into the light having convinced her that this was the right thing to do. She did this returning several minutes later and let us know that Sarah had gone on her journey into the light.

All that remained was for John to take the same path. However, this was somewhat more difficult and Karen had one hell of a fight trying to make him pass over. He was calling out the names of family members who we had not mentioned to Karen and whom Karen did not know, as he was fighting the inevitable. In the end she had to hold onto him herself until she got home so that she could call upon medium friends of her own to help her out. Collectively they managed to get John to pass into the light.

After those two days our lives could never ever be the same again. In the following days we learned that our families were also affected by the negative energy around us that we had fallen pray to. Charlotte's partner had been waking up in the night feeling as though he was being choked in the days leading up to this event and others had been suffering from mood swings. It had affected more than Sarah and I. We pieced together the events of those two days and realised that when we left the house, we were always meant to go to Sarah's Mom's house as this was who she would call out for in her time of need, just like Sarah Jenson did. We were meant to leave the bedroom lamp on because Sarah Jenson would have slept in fear of her Stepfather with a light on. And Sarah struggled to call out to her Mom with any volume that morning just as Sarah Jenson would have whilst being smothered.

There is thankfully a happy end to this story and I am told that both Sarah Jenson and John Berkshire are doing well and that Sarah has returned to the both of us as a Spirit Guide. She is grateful for the help she received and is now extremely happy. This was a delight to hear. No more was this beautiful fourteen year old Victorian girl suffering. She was now at peace and enjoying her life after death. As for John, he was apparently relieved to be on the other side and was in rehabilitation to help him learn from and come to terms with the injustices he carried out in his life.

In the days that followed it became apparent why Sarah had told us of her favourite colours pink and lilac. Sarah was constantly seeing these colours in sequence, whether by passing them in the street or seeing someone wearing them. Another of our friends, who is psychically aware once saw a pink and lilac diamond shaped light twinkling above Sarah's head. We know now that this is Sarah Jenson's calling card and that she uses this as a message to communicate to us that she is okay.

We both continue to feel her presence on a regular basis and a short while ago she left us an artificial pink and lilac flower in our house which appeared in the kitchen. We feel such a bond with Sarah Jenson and Sarah now refers to her as her 'spiritual sister'.

The artificial flower left inside our house by Sarah Jenson

This event had opened up something within us and although we had been thrown in at the deep end with this experience, there were plenty more beautiful and exciting ones to follow. As we know, everything happens for a reason! It had taken 159 years to resolve this matter but the light had finally shone on it bringing about its finale.

The whole thing was horrific at the time and it did scar us for some time afterwards. We sought some professional counselling to speed along our recovery and luckily with the help of those around us we made it. Everyone involved was now in a happier place and justice had been done.

And as for us, although temporarily damaged, we emerged like the Phoenix out of the ashes and onto a beautiful journey of spiritual experience filled with Love, Light and lots of Laughter!

CHAPTER 3: HEALING

We had been on such a journey with our spiritual experience so far but we know now that everything that happened was part of our spiritual awakening, forcing us to re-evaluate everything we knew, or thought we knew. Once we had gotten over the events that had taken place we could see that it had certainly served a number of purposes, one of those being that it had opened us up to the much wider reality that we all exist in. Naturally, one thing followed the other and before we knew it we had accumulated a wealth of spiritual experience which led us in search of our life purpose or soul mission. Sarah has found one of her purposes and this is in the undertaking of various healing techniques.

Healing can take place in various forms from the very physical, to the spiritual to even just 'being'. Sometimes without even realising we are emitting uplifting energy which goes to work on a deeper level of a person's being. Maybe just by smiling at someone in the street is enough to brighten up their day and in turn can lift their soul. Or maybe you practise a form of relaxation technique. Whatever it is we can heal in many ways and on many levels.

VIOLET FLAME.

We were introduced to a very effective healing tool called 'The Violet Flame'. This is a healing chant that was frequently used in days gone by, for instance in the Lost City of Atlantis. The Violet Flame is a spiritual fire of energy that vibrates at the colour of violet. This is the frequency that transmutes low energy to high, heavy to light and bad to good. It is miracle tool that anyone can use to bring about great changes in their life.

It works on every level of the being and it can heal you physically, emotionally, mentally and spiritually.

Human ego got in the way of this gift and it was eventually used for the wrong reasons. It was therefore taken away from humankind until they were once again ready to use it responsibly. It has now been returned to us and used wisely will bring about great change and transformation in a person's life. The Violet Flame was originally given to us by the Ascended Master Saint Germain and it is he who has voluntarily taken the responsibility for this return.

It was created to be used to heal oneself and the Earth by burning away anything that no longer serves. Whether Karma or addiction it is a powerful tool if used correctly. We attend Violet Flame meetings each month and use this gift to assist the Earth and its inhabitants and we are very often joined by Angels and Ascended Masters who can be heard decreeing with us and will then use the energy created for the good of all.

Shortly before this period of our lives Sarah felt an apparently out of the blue calling to learn the ancient form of healing known as Reiki, which she had received herself some time earlier in her life.

Reiki, (pronounced 'ray'-'key') is a Japanese word representing Universal Life Energy. Reiki is based on the belief that when spiritual energy is channelled through a Reiki practitioner, the patient's spirit is healed, which in turn heals the physical body. It is also used for the healing of the emotional, mental and etheric body and is a beautiful form of relaxation. This Universal life force energy will go to work on all the different levels of the being helping to remove blockages, negativities and will generally cleanse the body. Performed regularly Reiki can transform a person's life and miraculous results have been known to transpire as a result. Reiki can be used as an addition to traditional medicines and treatment and is completely harmless. It harnesses the energy of the Universe and the beauty is that it is available to all of us. You don't have to be a magician to enlist this beautiful energy as it is flowing through us all already. However, to use this healing ability today you would normally undergo an attunement to awaken and allow the energy to flow, allowing the recipient of this attunement to act as vessel. Reiki and similar healing forms are not limited to just humans either. It is available to be used on animals, trees, plants, homes, vehicles, food and drink. In fact, it can be used on just about anything. There are no limits.

Sarah explains her experience with Reiki:

"A couple of months before our experience in February, I suddenly had an overwhelming urge that I wanted to learn Reiki. I don't know where it came from but it certainly came with some gusto! So much so that I couldn't rest until I had identified somewhere near to our home that taught this ancient system.

I pondered over where I could go and searched the internet for local places. This took me a relatively short time as the first result I came across was for a place called 'The Cottage Healing Centre' which was ten minutes from our home. I just felt somehow I was being guided to do this as the feeling was persistent and I had a very excited energy in my stomach. I live by Mick's motto that if it feels right, then it probably is! I emailed the Cottage Healing Centre with my enquiry and to my amazement I received an email back within the hour. This confirmed that they did in fact attune people to Reiki at the Cottage and that I would be put in touch with the most appropriate person. Shortly afterwards I had a telephone call from Sue Orchard, one of the Cottage founders and a Reiki master teacher. She explained to me what Reiki entailed and that she worked closely with the Angelic realm and had actually seen an Angel with her physical eyes. This was all quite new to me but I liked what I was hearing. It just felt right. Sue explained that I was most welcome to come in and meet her at the Cottage to get a feel for her and the place to make sure it was right for me. I didn't need to. I just knew by speaking to Sue on the phone that she was the person and the Cottage was the place, odd really as I hadn't seen either. I trusted what I today know as my intuition and went with it, just knowing that I was being taken by the hand and guided towards something special.

Without further adieu I booked my course with Sue for two weeks later. I couldn't wait. The feeling didn't go away having slept on it for all that time. I arrived at the Cottage Healing Centre two weeks later to commence my two day Reiki Level One course. There I was to meet my Reiki tutor and cottage co-founder Sue. There felt a strong and deep bond between the two of us that seemed so familiar as if we had known each other from a lifetime past. However, this was definitely the first time that we had met, in this lifetime at least.

The cottage Healing centre had a beautiful and friendly atmosphere and I knew I had found a sanctuary where I could express myself without any fear of ridicule. Everyone was a like minded soul and I felt instantly at peace and very comfortable. It had a feeling of 'home'.

The course began with an Angel card reading to enlist the help and guidance of the Angelic realm and for them to assist in this wondrous communion. This was followed by the introduction by Sue of the Angels and of the Goddess energy, also present with us on this auspicious occasion. Sue explained to me the importance of balancing masculine and feminine energy and where there is a God, there is also a Goddess. This beautiful balance of Yin and Yang in all things will make for a happy and fulfilled life nurturing the qualities of both ends of the spectrum. This was a beautiful start and I had learned so much already. We continued with a series of attunements where I would sit or lie down in a relaxed state and then meditate whilst Sue would perform her role around me.

Following one of these attunements my Reiki master allowed me to sit in meditation alone. The room was dark and there was gentle music playing helping me to keep in the zone! I opened my eyes for a few seconds, feeling completely relaxed and allowed myself to stare into nothingness. All of a sudden there was a huge flash of white light which lit up the wall to my right. It quickly disappeared and I began feeling tingly and goosepimply although still very relaxed. I could feel a presence around me but I had no idea who or what this was.

A short time later Sue returned to see how I had got on. I told her about the flash of white light to which she smiled knowingly and said "How amazing, that's the Angels". She explained some of the different signs that can be seen or felt when Angels are around and these included flashes of light and feeling tingly and goosepimply amongst other things. White feathers are another common calling card of this beloved realm. I was amazed. I had never been opposed to the belief in these magnificent beings but I now knew that they were for real.

I completed my Reiki level one course the following day which was again a complete joy. I had told Mick all about my experiences and at the end of day two asked him to come in and meet the Cottage clan! He too felt instantly at ease and loved the ambience of the place. Although he didn't have any urges to do any of the courses or to have any treatments he suddenly felt a sense of purpose and a longing to be there. We knew we had found the Cottage Healing Centre for a reason and looking back now, I can see that the doors where opened for us by a higher existence.

We both now spend quite a lot of our time at the Cottage attending various workshops and events amongst other things and soaking up the wonderful energies during the social gatherings. One thing I can honestly say having settled into the environment and knowing everyone is that spiritual people are definitely not boring"!

Sarah has since completed her Reiki level two, practitioner level and now conducts healing sessions with the Cottage being her base. The events in our life had opened up our dormant abilities and both Sarah and I now regularly experience psychic phenomena as well as intuitively guided messages. This was apparent when shortly before completing her Reiki level two course, Sarah once again felt the overwhelming urge to pursue this sudden motivation. She explained to me that she just knew that it was time. This feeling had again come from out of the blue but she just knew that she was being guided onto the next step of her journey.

After booking the course Sarah explained to me some intuitive feelings she was getting about the whole thing. She said that she knew that when she was at practitioner level, that she needed to conduct healing just one day a week at the Cottage. She also said that she was getting through that this day needed to be a Wednesday. Pretty random I know, but she trusted the guidance she was being given and so did I. Not only that, she was also receiving a message about conducting Angel card readings as part of her sessions. She'd never before conducted an Angel card reading for anyone but knew that everything was in hand! It seemed everything had all been set out for her and all that remained was to first complete the course! "Let's book it", I told her. I knew that all of the detail Sarah had been intuitively given was for a reason.

Sarah went onto complete the course which was again conducted by Reiki Master Sue.

I was with Sarah immediately after the course where we spoke with Sue. Sarah enquired about becoming a therapist with the Cottage. Sue smiled a knowing smile and explained that she had been getting a message which turned out to be identical to what Sarah had been given only days earlier. Sue said one day a week would be good and that Wednesday would be ideal. Sarah and I looked at each other in wonderment and laughed at the accuracy of Sue's intuition. Sarah explained to Sue that this was what she was being given from above. Sue paused for a moment and then asked Sarah "Have you thought about doing Angel card readings as well". Again we laughed, "Well funnily enough" Sarah replied, overcome with astonishment "That's exactly what I've been getting".

Ironically this kind of session was not yet offered at the Cottage and so it seemed another piece of the spiritual jigsaw was coming together. Amazing how it all comes together when something is meant to be!

CHAPTER 4: ANGELS, GUIDES & ASCENDED MASTERS

ANGELS.

Until Sarah completed her Reiki course we hadn't really any interest in the Angelic realm. It was only when we had been introduced to them by our newly discovered spiritual friends that we actually began to start taking notice. Now, I know only too well that lots of people scoff at the idea of a powerful presence like the Angels really existing but for Sarah and I, they are part of our everyday life. Everyday we call upon them in one form or another, both for protection and guidance and even just to feel their wondrous presence.

In fact, you can call upon these beloved beings for absolutely anything and they are only ever too happy to help. For example, have you ever tried calling upon the car parking Angel?! "The car parking Angel" I hear you ask?! Now not everyone agrees with calling on a car parking Angel as they believe that the Angels have more important tasks to be getting on with. However, Angels vowed to serve humanity and they wish to help you in any way they can and if that means making a parking space available, then it will be done. Try it. It works. If the Angels can perform a simple task that in turn makes your life easier then they want to help. Your Angels are standing by just waiting to be let in. In reality they are already assisting in everyday life it's just that many people don't realise it and so a lot of their work may go unnoticed. But when you begin to understand and work with this beautiful realm, great things transpire. The Angels are a force to be reckoned with and every action they perform comes out of Love.

The Angels will never force anything upon you. They are beings of Love and purity who hold no judgement and they respect our freewill. However they can only help you if you ask them. They can open up certain avenues and doorways if it is part of your path but even then the decision to take that help lies with you. We are ultimately in control of our own lives and destinies.

Many Angels can replicate themselves so if they are called upon or needed in multiple places at any given time, not necessarily just on this planet, they can make themselves available. That is why there is no job too small for an Angel as they can help all who call for them at the same time. You may not realise it but they are the perfect friends that have been with you all along. And boy is it a momentous occasion for all when they are acknowledged.

There are several types of Angels that have specific areas of expertise. For example the Archangels are the overseers of both the Angels and our Guardian Angels.

There are seven main Archangels all who have divine feminine counterparts or twin flames. They can undertake any task but each has their own specialised roles. They are:

Jophiel & Christine (Yellow Ray) Qualities = Wisdom, Understanding, Enlightenment, Illumination.

Raphael & Mother Mary (Green Ray) Qualities = Healing, Truth, Abundance, Science, Constancy.

Michael & Faith (Blue Ray) Qualities = Communication, Power, Strength, Divine Will, Protection.

Chamuel & Charity (Pink Ray) Qualities = Love, Creativity, Beauty, Compassion, Discernment.

Uriel & Aurora (Purple, Gold & Ruby Ray) Qualities = Service, Brotherhood, Peace, Justice, Conquering fear

Zadkiel & Holy Amethyst (Violet Ray) Qualities = Freedom, Change, Healing, Manifestation.

Gabriel & Hope (White Ray) Qualities = Discipline, Purity, Honour, Hope, Wholeness.

There are many other Archangels who have not been covered in this book whom have a vital role in Earthly affairs and the ascension of mankind. Call upon the specific Archangel mentioned for help in any of the areas listed.

Guardian Angels are those that walk with us at all times in everyday life and were 'assigned' to be with us all throughout our lives from the point of birth to the point of physical death. They are beautiful beings and Sarah and I are fortunate enough to have been able to get to know ours. Some might say that if Guardian Angels existed then no one would get hurt or killed. Not so. Remember that we are all on our divine paths and before incarnation into our lives we set out a timetable of events to occur so that our souls and or others can learn and grow. As previously mentioned we also have freewill which our Angels will not interfere with as decreed by Divine law. So they will help and assist us to a point but the decision must be our own. There are exceptions to the rule of course, for example when faced with physical danger and it is not a person's time to die, it has been known that Guardian Angels will intervene and help to change the course of events. There are many such recorded examples of this.

In early 2009 we were introduced to Richard Keogh the 'Angelman'. Richard had been involved in this subject from a very young age and has the ability to see the Angelic realm as well as other wondrous beings from the elemental kingdom including Fairies, Elves, Gnomes, Tree Spirits and many others who learn and grow by observing Human behavioural patterns. This also includes the animal kingdom.

Sarah and I went to one of Richard's events in which he was to tune in and draw our Guardian Angels for us. So we arrived one sunny afternoon and individually sat down. Sarah went first and closed her eyes whilst Richard tuned in and drew her Guardian Angel. Sarah had asked her Guardian to show them self to her as well so she could see for herself. She did see an image flash in front of her mind's eye and to her amazement Richard had drawn the exact same image.

The Angel was a large and powerful protector, who has a strong love for Sarah and was around during the time of Atlantis, in which both Sarah and I have had past lives. Sarah's Guardian would not give her his name. This was her challenge to find out for herself by whatever means available to her, most likely through meditation.

Sarah's Guardian Angel:

Sarah was told that her Guardian was holding a clear quartz crystal that she needed to find. This crystal would be holding much knowledge and many memories from her own days in Atlantis. We have since found this beautiful crystal which is covered shortly in more detail.

After many months of seeking his identity, through meditation Sarah eventually discovered that her Guardian's name is 'Corey'. This in Hebrew means 'God's Peace'.

I went in next and my Guardian was also drawn. My Guardian is a female and she too is Atlantean. Just like Sarah I had to discover her name for myself through meditation.

She was holding a chalice or Holy Grail which suggested that I had connections to the Knights of old. The chalice also symbolises the opening up of the heart and allowing the divine feminine aspect of ones self to flow. Richard told me that there was a second Guardian Angel with me who was a strong masculine warrior Angel. However he did not need to present himself on this occasion as at that time I was already aware of this masculine, warrior like side of myself.

Again after much time and patience I have learned that my Guardian's name is 'Michaela', which in Hebrew means 'Who is like God' and is the female version of the name Michael.

Michaela wanted me to open up to the Goddess within and begin to nurture the female qualities that we all possess, such as intuition, creativity and nurturing itself. For this reason Michaela was the Angel that most wanted to come forward and connect with me to help me to learn and understand and in turn balance my divine masculine and feminine.

We both continue to interact with our Guardian Angels on a daily basis and work closely with them.

Michael's guardian Angel:

As previously mentioned Sarah's Guardian Angel, Corey, had given her a message to try to find the clear quartz Atlantean crystal that he was holding. It would be one that was big enough to have to cup in both hands and had a shimmering sparkle to it with rainbow effects throughout. It was also holding doorways to ancient knowledge that was waiting to be unlocked with memories of lifetimes past. Some months later Sarah found this crystal on eBay! Brand new it had been recently mined from a cave in Brazil. This is the crystal:

Sarah describes the event of finding the crystal like this:

"As soon as I saw the beautiful clear quartz crystal I knew that it was the one. I'd been searching eBay for many hours over many days as well as looking in shops. I had seen many similar but nothing had the effect on me that this crystal had. My stomach turned with excitement, our computer ceased to function properly momentarily, my phone switched itself off! All in the space of me clicking on the 'buy it now' button! I wasn't going to let this one get away. The energy had already started to work its magic. It felt like a reunion of old friends that hadn't seen each other for years, (14,000 to be exact)! The energy was frantic as though a party was getting underway! Crystals are powerful entities that are also part of the elemental kingdom.

They are living beings that have potential far beyond our current understanding, but thankfully, this knowledge is beginning to make itself known to us once again. All in divine timing!

I am so thankful for being reunited with this crystal. Now it comes everywhere with us, even to bed! Amazing things have taken place since being with the crystal and it is like our little baby that we are proud to be connected with".

ASCENDED MASTERS:

Ascended masters have had many lifetimes on this Earth at various points in history. They led good lives and more importantly made good choices and learned from any mistakes addressing all Karmic issues. They learned to control all emotions and this led them to the mastering of life, maintaining their connection to the creator.

These masters are famous even today, but have sometimes been known by different identities. There are many masters all of whom lived on Earth and eventually ascended. Ascended Masters are excellent guides and spiritual teachers and healers.

The masters are powerful guides with whose help you will be closer to understanding your life's purpose. If there are significant changes to be made in your life, the masters can help you to courageously carry these out. They can also help you to develop your spiritual abilities such as psychic and manifestation powers.

The masters each have their own area of speciality, for instance, Jesus is a master healer. Other masters are responsible for ascension, manifestation and relationships amongst other roles. They are not bound by any religion and like the Angels will help anyone who may call upon them regardless of background or belief.

Here are a few of the ascended masters we have been privileged enough to have personally come across on our journey and I have no doubt that the numbers will increase at the right time:

Jesus.

Jesus is one of the most famous historical characters especially when it comes to Christianity. Jesus gave us a message of Love and forgiveness and he let us witness many demonstrations of miraculous healings and manifestations, the turning of water to wine for example.

It may be surprising to know that Jesus helps anyone who calls upon him and he too is not bound by the person's religious or spiritual beliefs, and has no restrictions. You can call upon Jesus for help with healing yourself or others, emotionally, physically or mentally at any time.

Saint Germain.

Saint Germain is a count from the French region of St Germain and is not a catholic saint as many consider him to be. He was called the wonderman of Europe during his lifetime in the early 1700's. Saint Germain demonstrated many magical abilities and gave gems and fountain-of- youth-like elixirs to his many friends.

He was a virtuoso musician and linguist who was loved by royalty and blue collar workers alike. Saint Germain helps light workers who seek world peace and who want to bring about integrity and honesty in governmental and other systems.

Kwan Yin.

Kwan Yin is the Buddhist Goddess of compassion whose name means 'She who hears all prayers'. She will give a cloak of invisibility for light workers so that they can remain invisible to dark forces whilst carrying out their work.

At her mortal death Kwan Yin rejected Buddhahood and elected to stay close to Earth and help humankind until such a time arises where everyone will become enlightened and on the road to ascension. You can call upon Kwan Yin for help with forgiveness and compassion. She works in a gentle and loving way.

Mother Mary.

Mother Mary is the Mother of Jesus and is pure and compassionate. Mary helps children (Including our inner children) and caretakers of children. If your life purpose is to help children Mother Mary can be asked for help and guidance.

Paul the Venetian.

Paul the Venetian was the Italian renaissance Artist Paolo Caliari (His last name was later changed to Veronese to signify his birth place of Verona). He moved to Venice in the 1500's during the cities golden era (Which is why he is now called the Venetian).

There he painted Religious Murals and paintings. He successfully defended himself against charges of blasphemy during the inquisition for his artistic version of the last supper. You can call upon Paul the Venetian for help with artistic expression and creativity.

Serapis Bey.

Serapis Bey is an Egyptian God of ascension and a bridge between Heaven and Earth. He is a great motivator and life coach who motivates people to take good care of themselves physically, spiritually and emotionally. You can call upon Serapis Bey for additional energy and motivation to take action.

Serapis Bey is also the master who will take you for the ascension test. He appears stern but I am told he has a great sense of humour! If you come across him in your life, either through meditation or dreams, then be nice! I have seen him a number of times in meditation but I'm not sure if this was for any tests... At least I hope not!

There are many other ascended masters whom have the same goal to help mankind. There are too many to mention but all are intriguing nevertheless and I hope that you will also identify and work with these great masters during your own lifetime.

Ascended masters like the Angels each have an individual aroma that makes you aware of their presence and of course when you get to know that aroma you can distinguish who it is that is visiting you. We have had numerous beautiful smells in our house that have continuously reappeared periodically and remained with us for a short time. I have counted at least six different aromas at home in recent months. As yet we have not worked out who these visitors are but with a little more meditation I would hope that one day soon we will discover the answers.

Many people who are on this path will have a master close by working with them. This can be interchangeable depending on the individuals needs at any given time. At the time of writing I am currently working with St Germain and Sarah is working closely with Paul the Venetian. Both represent amongst many other things, artistic expression. This is a very creative and expressive time in both our lives so this seems to fit nicely for us to have these particular masters working with us.

We don't know where this is taking us but I know it is going to be beneficial to us and very fascinating.

GUIDES.

All of us have spirit guides whether or not you are religious or spiritual, the only difference is when you are spiritual you are aware of these guides and other beings around you.

Both Sarah and I have a number of guides at this time. Guides can change if need be at various points of your life depending on where we are and what we need at that particular period.

I currently have a healing monk working with me whose identity I am still seeking. Sarah Jenson as previously mentioned has returned to both Sarah and I as a guide as well as our cosmic being from Sirius named Amanda. Amanda is part of the Ashtar Command Galactic Federation of Light star ship fleet who are covered in more detail later on.

One night in August of 2009 Sarah was outside with the front door open and I heard a female voice say "Babe". This sounded like Sarah and so I went outside to see what she wanted. Sarah insisted that she had not spoken or called me but I found out the next day that she had heard this same voice calling. I had heard the same voice once before and again thought it was Sarah calling me from the shower but Sarah knew nothing about it.

It is a special feeling when you hear a voice from another dimension that has entered your own. I was determined to find out who this voice belonged to. We had recently completed an input on using a dowser otherwise known as a pendulum. These can be used to identify energies as well as to connect you with your guides and higher self for example. This can be done by ensuring that the dowser is protected with light and then by asking a question either mentally or aloud. The dowser or pendulum will then respond by either moving around in a circular motion left or right indicating a 'yes' or 'no' answer or will swing side to side or remain stationary. This can mean that the dowser is working and in consideration. I used my dowser to find out the identity of the voice we had heard. The conversation went as follows:

(Yes & No check made)

Me: Was that my guide who myself and Sarah heard last night?

D: Yes

Me: Do we have the same guides?

D: Yes

Me: Are we a team on the same mission?

D: Yes

At that point the name 'Amanda' popped into my head seemingly from out of nowhere.

Me: Is my guide named Amanda?

D: Yes

Me: Is my guide named Cedric? (Just testing)!

D: No

Me: Is she from the Angelic realm?

D: No

Me: Is she a family member? (As in a passed relative)

D: No

Me: Is she a Cosmic Being?

D: Yes

Me: Is she from Ashtar Command?

D: Yes

Me: Is she from the Pleiades?

D: No

This time the word 'Sirius' popped into my head.

Me: Is Amanda from Sirius

D: Yes

Me: Will I be getting to know her better?

D: Yes

End of dowser session.

We all have Angels, Guides and Masters around us just waiting to be called into action so that they can be a part of our lives. Now that we have allowed ours to be a part of ours, a beautiful relationship has ensued. Our advice to others would be to let theirs in for an exciting and fulfilling journey! There is no better feeling than to see or hear a celestial guide and it will be a totally amazing experience for both you and them. We can only imagine the party they must have thrown when we finally woke up!

CHAPTER 5: CELESTIAL VISITATION

As mentioned in the previous chapter, when you are able to tune into the frequency of the celestial beings, it is a magnificent and wondrous feeling. It is something that works on both levels though. When you have raised your vibration enough you will be able to lift yourself into the other dimensions and make the connection, just as these beautiful beings do for us however they must lower their vibrations so as to meet us in the middle.

Visitation from our spiritual guides and teachers can take form in many shapes and sizes! For example, you may hear a spoken word or sentence in your inner ear, you may see mental images in your mind's eye or you may be fortunate enough to be able to see them with your physical sight. You may get a visit through someone else like when having a spiritual reading of some kind.

ARCHANGEL RAPHAEL.

A story that still makes me smile even to this day took place when Sarah and I went to a spiritual event not too far away from home a short time ago. I had in the days leading up to this event been having a bit of 'stick' shall we say from Sarah about my diet. I knew she was being influenced by Archangel Raphael, and so did she which made it all the more fun for her! Archangel Raphael is the healing Angel who promotes healthful eating and drinking.

I thought that I had weathered that particular storm quite well in the circumstances, since Raphael had used my Wife to give me hassle. For my own good though! Anyway I attended this event and we decided that we wanted an Angel card reading. I chose one card and Sarah chose two. As soon as the cards were revealed one of Sarah's choices was... guess who? You got it. Archangel Raphael! Well you can imagine how I just knew what was coming next!!

The card reader started laughing to herself and pointed at Sarah and said "You chose this card, but it's a message for him", pointing at me with the Raphael card in her hand! The reader said that they, meaning whoever was being channelled at that time by her had placed an image of a hamburger into her head and wanted me to eat more fresh fruit and vegetables so I could give my body the nutrients it needed.

We both found this hilarious due to the fact that every time Sarah and I ate out, which was quite often, I would always order a burger! Yet again the message had found its way through the shield of denial and had reached me loud and clear.

My eating habits have since changed and I do now eat lots of fruit and vegetables and out of respect for animals both Sarah and I have completely given up eating meat of any kind. We have learned that each animal has a life and soul of its own and a personality to go with it. They have as much right to live as we. It is important however to acknowledge that not everyone is in the same place as ourselves when it comes to this subject and it is the individuals own personal choice as to what they eat. Everyone has a free will and free choice and it was under that same free will that we made our conscious decision not to eat meat again. There are many substitutes out there.

ARCHANGEL MICHAEL.

One evening in July 2009 at 10pm Sarah and I were at home playing cards on the sofa. We were facing opposite directions. The TV was not on and the room was twilight with there being barely any light at all. It had been a stressful few days for us with various things taking place and I had privately in my mind asked for some sort of presence to confirm that we had help in our time of need.

Within a minute of saying this to myself there was an almighty explosion in the centre of the room which lit up the whole living room.

As this happened I looked up to face the explosion and as I did I saw a large but beautiful blue orb of energy behind Sarah. It had an awesome authoritative presence about it which made me feel like bowing my head. The orb was about twelve inches in diameter and remained stationary in mid air in the centre of the room for about four or five seconds before disappearing. This was an "I AM here" statement. Both myself and Sarah immediately began to feel tingly all over and were covered with a pins and needles sensation from head to toe indicating that this great presence had entered our energy fields.

We both knew that this mighty orb was the wonderful Archangel Michael, a seven feet wonder, warrior and protector Angel whom we have both been working with for a short time now. When he is close by we often come over in a hot flush as he enters our energy fields. This was the first time I had seen a form of him appear with my own eyes. Although I had felt this powerful presence on many occasions before, this visit was beyond words. I was humbled and honoured and it gave me a sense of all is and will be ok. In times of trouble or when you just need that little extra helping of confidence ask for this Archangel and the sensation you get from his nearness alone gives you all the backbone, confidence and protection that you need helping you to face anything.

Archangel Michael had appeared to me in one of my first meditations and he was dressed in a white robe. I could not see his face because of the bright light shining from him. It was only later on when I saw a picture of the same being with the same white robe and bright shimmering light on a picture board that I realised who it was that had appeared to me during my meditation.

A few months after this vision I was at a spiritual gathering and as part of one of the exercises involving feeling energy, we had to walk towards our partner of the night. This was the first time I had met and spoken with my partner. We slowly walked towards each other with our eyes closed and arms outstretched feeling for the energy, stopping a few feet away from each other. After I had reached my partner she said that as I was walking towards her she could see a large male dressed in a white robe behind me whose face she could not see because it was covered by a bright white light making it impossible for her to see who it was. I was astonished! This was exactly how I had seen Archangel Michael in the meditation months earlier. Only Sarah knew what I had seen before this so it was excellent confirmation that I had been visited rather that just putting it down to imagination.

Both Sarah and I feel a close bond with Archangel Michael and know that we are 'Blue Ray' protectors ourselves. I know that we are right alongside Michael fighting for the light and for the good of all. Spreading the Love and the light is one of our purposes and we continue to do this with grace.

WHITE FEATHERS.

Angels are always around us, whether they are our guardians or are general servers of mankind. When you ask them for a sign you often get a reply in the form of a white feather as a reassurance, an "I am around" confirmation. This is one of their unique signatures and calling cards. There are plenty of amazing stories out there whereby people have received a feather following calling upon an Angel.

We started to receive feathers during our times of need a short period ago helping us to keep going in our endeavours. These feathers served as a sign of the Angels presence and gave us the courage and conviction we needed to make significant changes in our lives. Some of the White feathers have been placed on our door step, some actually wedged underneath the door frame or even on the pavement by our house on a route that we always take when exiting.

I have even seen one drift passed the window of our house and then land on the window ledge, appearing from nowhere. We sometimes see them land in the middle of the road in front of us whilst driving. Until we embarked upon our journey I never saw white feathers at the best of times but now we see them as messages of encouragement in response to our calls for guidance.

The most amazing feather incident happened to us one day when we were having breakfast at a local cafe in our Town. We were sat at a table outside adjacent to other tables with other customers. It was a beautiful day with a bright sunny sky. There was nothing more around us other than shops and concrete. Both Sarah and I just happened to look up and as we did, saw a white feather falling from the sky. It was about four feet from the table when I first saw it, drifting towards us. The feather gently landed on our table and rested in between myself & Sarah. We looked at each other in amazement and laughed out loud at the prominence of this feather's appearance.

Pictured below are some of the feathers sent to us by the Angelic realm:

In addition to white feathers we very often see flashes of light especially at home that come and go in an instant. These flashes of light come in many colours but are equally pleasurable to the eye and they let us know that Angels are around us all the time. These flashes are Angels showing a presence in a visual yet unmistakable way and it appears that if you acknowledge them and communicate with them they appear more and more. Angels want to serve you but need your permission to help and intervene on this free will planet that we inhabit. Angels grow and develop themselves by service to humankind and what's more they Love us, you will never find a more genuine and unselfish friend who only has your best interest at heart.

SPIRITS.

Many of our experiences have also involved past relatives and family members now on the other side and it almost seems as if they sometimes queue up to speak with you wherever there is an opening.

Following a small group meditation one night in August, I was told by the class conductor that I had a presence standing next to me. He got the feeling it was a Grandfather figure. He went on to tell me a little about this presence in order to jog my memory, telling me that this energy was hard working, loved his garden, smoked, cut his tobacco up with a knife and always patted you on the back when greeting you. I understood this to be my grandfather Bill Harris who passed in the early eighties.

He told me that he had a message for me which was "You're doing well son". This made me feel somewhat proud and humbled to know he was still around and thought so well of me.

We were very close and I was always told that I was the apple of his eye. He had fought in the 2nd world war in the Black Watch Regiment and had seen action in North Africa with Monty's (field marshal Montgomery) Desert Rats and at Dunkirk. He would have seen some terrible things and his numerous medals where testament to that fact, but he was a humble man who never sought any title of heroism.

Our clairvoyant skills are developing but they are not at any advanced levels by any means at this stage of our path. I know this gift will come in good time for the both of us when it is the right time as part of our development. But nevertheless both Sarah and I have seen, and continue to see spirits around us.

One time at work in the early hours of the morning I went into a toilet on the top floor. It was dark and there were no lights on in the corridors. I noticed the end cubicle was closed but there was no one in there. I listened for a while but there was no noise. There was complete silence and I was definitely alone in there. As I left the toilet and made my way back out to the corridor letting the door shut behind me I could see the silhouette of a person standing behind the glass window of the main toilet door. There was the head and shoulders of someone but I was definitely alone there. I made my way to the end of the corridor but no one came out behind me.

On other occasions when out shopping I have seen figures walk past me, but on turning to face them, there has been no one there. This often happens to Sarah too. This is because we are now both at a stage of spiritual development where our third eye chakra is opening up and becoming clear. The third eye chakra is the energy centre based on our forehead in between our physical eyes which governs spiritual vision and other such like abilities. Anyone can learn to develop but it is something that will come naturally when on the spiritual path.

In July 2009 we went on a visit to Wiltshire in the UK where we stayed in a beautiful small country pub hotel. Our room was on the ground floor with patio doors opening out onto a wonderful large field where farm animals wondered. On one particular sunny day I was watching a lone sheep in the field. The sheep was probably no-more than fifty feet away from me, grazing in the grass. All of a sudden I saw a deep grey mist appear next to the sheep. It rose like the smoke from a grass fire and I knew that it was an apparition. The mist moved off with control and disappeared after about a minute and a half or so. This mist was the size of an adult male but due to my clairvoyant abilities not being fully open yet, I could not see enough to witness any features of the man.

It was suggested to me that this may have been the spirit of an old farmer still tending to his sheep even after his own passing. This explanation seemed to fit what I had seen. Interesting that some souls even after they have passed on still can't bring themselves to let go of the physical reality.

One day myself and Sarah were outside in our front garden. Sarah's attention was suddenly drawn towards a man she had seen walking towards another row of cars near to our own car. This took Sarah by surprise as the man, she said, appeared from nowhere and she had to quickly take a second glance but when she looked around again within seconds, there was no-one there. The figure had just disappeared. We naturally had a good look around to see if we could find anyone perhaps hiding behind cars but there wasn't a trace!

On a Clairvoyance theme one late Saturday evening I was at home on the sofa, one of my favourite past times! Suddenly I had an image boldly appear in my mind's eye. The image was of a passed relative named Mick, my auntie's father.

In the next thirty seconds or so I found myself having a conversation with Mick. It was like I had switched onto autopilot and was being engaged in mind to mind communication. The conversation was entirely about a message that I was once given from Mick via Karen the medium and which he had wanted me to pass on to his Wife and Daughter. The message was that he had passed over to the other side without any problems and that he was okay. He wanted them to stop grieving for him and for them to know that he was still with them.

I had asked another member of family to pass this message on as I didn't see these individuals very often. It was only recently that I learned that the message had not yet been given due to the sensitivity of the subject. Obviously it is sometimes a difficult thing to give anyone a message depending on the nature, but even more so when it is a message from the other side!

Mick had come through to me to let me know that he still wanted the message to be given. I promised him that it would be and my last words to him were "Take care", unusual I know considering where he is now. I remember coming back to reality following this conversation and telling Sarah all about it, who told me she had been looking at me wondering why I was staring into oblivion and looking rather white!

CHILDREN.

It is important to mention that children, especially between the ages of 0-7 years are very psychic and imaginary friends may not be so imaginary after all! It's even more important that their gift is not stifled or suppressed in any way and they should be allowed to develop and express themselves accordingly. Basically, it wasn't that long ago that they came from spirit and so they are born into this world with their full senses still intact. It is only after time within some of the rigid structures and systems of today, such as school, that these abilities start to diminish and lay dormant awaiting re-activation. Our children are constantly bombarded with left brain stuff, which is the side of the brain that is rigid and likes structure. The right side however, is the 'out there' side of the brain that doesn't like structure and wants to be freely creative and expressive and to connect to all that is on a deeper level. We should have a healthy balance between the two but unfortunately a lot of systems today mainly concentrate on the left side. The brain is a powerful computer and is capable of reaching into other dimensions and realities allowing you to interact with the spiritual world. Children are so innocent so when they do interact with the other realms, it feels very natural to them and they see no cause for concern.

Sarah can remember a number of occasions from when she was very young where she was visited by other realms, some of which still stand out to her today as she explains below:

"The earliest memory I have of the spirit world happened when I was around one year old. It's amazing to be able to remember that far back but I remember the event like it was yesterday.

My Mom took my sister Charlotte and I to visit family on an estate not too far from our own. There we were greeted by my Auntie and Cousins. We all went and sat in the living room and I was placed onto the floor to bum shuffle around! Whilst performing this interesting manoeuvre I noticed a man I knew to be my Uncle Paddy standing over by the rear window of the living room area. He had big dark curly hair and appeared to be checking on his family. He smiled at me and I responded in my native baby tongue that only I could understand! I don't remember seeing him again following that day and believed he had passed away a few years later.

Some years later my Mom and me were looking through our photo box and she pulled out a photograph of this same Uncle. I recognised him instantly and said to Mom "Oh yes, I remember him". A concerned look developed across her face and she began questioning me asking "Paddy, you've seen Paddy"? I nodded and she said "You couldn't have, he died before you were born".

Well I wasn't expecting that. I had seen him clear as day and I just knew who he was. I described to my Mom when and where I saw my Uncle and she told me that Paddy lost his life some three years before my birth. Paddy was easily identifiable because of his big hair! My Mom, although a little confused, knew I was telling the truth as everything I said to her seemed to fit. We still talk about it to this day and live in the knowledge that Paddy is still around, checking in on everyone from time to time".

Paddy has made himself known on a number of occasions since Sarah's experience. He had been around the three of us at the time of the Sarah Jenson experience and had been talking with Kate for forty minutes during the journey back with Karen the medium.

One evening recently before the publication of this book, myself, Sarah and her mother Kate where sitting in the conservatory of Kate's house following a night out at a local Indian restaurant to celebrate Kate's birthday. It was around 10pm and we had got onto the subject of the paranormal and our experiences of it. In particular we were talking about the story of Paddy, Sarah's Uncle and Kate's brother. Paddy's life was taken from him in 1980 at around midnight on a Saturday night into a Sunday morning.

Kate suddenly sat up to attention and turned to both myself and Sarah. She asked "Did you hear that cough"? She was indicating that it had come from the room adjacent which was empty at that time. We didn't hear any noise. Kate was adamant she had just heard a cough and it sounded very familiar to her. Kate said that she recognised it from somewhere and both Sarah and I started to feel tingly as we do when spirit and other energies enter our energy fields. Kate then acknowledged that it was Paddy's cough. We knew that he was with us again. I had only ever seen a photograph of Paddy but although we could feel his nearness, Sarah and I knew that this was a visit for Kate.

The strangest part to this was when we all looked up at the television on Kate's conservatory wall. There we saw in green letters and numerals the characters *00:00 SUN* written across the screen. Kate looked bewildered and told us that the time and date settings had never been used on this television and had never appeared on the screen. The television was some years old and belonged to Sarah when she was a teenager. Apart from this, it was Monday. Then it suddenly dawned on Kate that this was in fact around the time and day that Paddy passed over, (00:00 Sunday). To add to this already interesting event, almost immediately after this connection was made, the television returned to normal and this time, there were no time or date displayed.

All sensations of this visit then disappeared as speedily as it had appeared. It was definitely a visit from this family member letting us know that he was there. As it was Kate's birthday I believe Paddy had come to wish his Sister a happy birthday and his presence was a timely visit to recognise this special day.

We have learned that if you speak about a family member who is in spirit they will come and be with you. It had happened once again on this occasion and even as I write we are feeling all of the usual traits of a visitation and know that Paddy is here again!

Another visitation that Sarah remembers with great fondness occurred a very short time later and has left her wanting to reconnect with these Heavenly visitors. Once again Sarah explains:

"On a number of occasions and at one point almost every night while around two to three years old, I would be visited whilst in bed at night. My Mom or Dad would tell me it was bed time and like any other child of that age I would do my best to fight it! They always won and eventually I would be carried upstairs and into my bedroom where I was placed into bed. Following a short story or lullaby my Mom and Dad would wish me a goodnight, switch off the lights and shut the door. That's when the visitors came.

The room was dark and quiet and I waited for a minute or two. Then all of a sudden the most amazing sight would appear before me. Through my bedroom window came flying several beautiful coloured orbs of lights. They ranged from light green, light blue, yellow and pink and were all beautiful pastel colours. They seemed to be the size of a tennis ball and they came gently meandering around me. I would sit up and watch in excitement as these beautiful lights orbited around me. Happily I reached out to them and laughed as they zipped around my room.

Then they would leave me. Gently they took the same path disappearing out of the window. I also vaguely remember the presence of an angel who would be with me and talking to me before saying "Goodnight" and leaving with the orbs.

One day I saw a television programme about fireflies. I watched as the bottom halves of the fireflies lit up brightly and so I began associating these with the orbs of light. I started telling my Mom and Dad that the 'fireflies' had been to see me again. They thought nothing more of it assuming that the lights I was talking about were a dream or in my imagination. One night, whilst travelling in the car my firefly friends paid me an unexpected visit. It was dark and I was sat in the rear passenger seat. I was still very young, around four or five. I looked out of the window to my left to see four or five beautiful coloured orbs flying alongside my window. Once again these beautiful pastel coloured orbs had found me. Green, Pink, Blue and yellow, they really were divine. Unflustered and being used to these celestial beings I said across the seat to my Mom "Mom, the fireflies are flying next to the car". I saw her look over her shoulder from the seat in front of me, trying to see if she could see spot the mysterious lights I kept referring to. She couldn't see anything and asked me "I can't see them, are they still"? "Yes" I replied. My Mother continued to look intently outside of our moving vehicle but could not see the orbs.

Now, all these years later I have spoken about this to my both my Mom and Dad who still remember me mentioning the 'fireflies'. I explained to them exactly what I used to see and that it definitely wasn't a dream or my imagination! I now know that these orbs were my Heavenly guides, most likely my Angels who would stop by and check in on me. I feel absolutely blessed to be able to remember these extraordinary phenomena and know that there will be plenty more where that came from".

On the theme of Celestial visits, many of the great composers based their work on music they had heard during a period between sleep and consciousness and copied it. This is known as the 'Music of the Spheres'.

Sarah has also had such an experience where she was in that place of the space in between, between sleep and wakefulness. She described to me how one morning just before waking up she could hear what she described as lovely music of a Native American Indian origin. She explained how this enchanting sound went on for about three minutes. She could hear a Chief like voice chanting, accompanied by music and instruments that she didn't recognise. This appeared to her to be by her side in the bedroom having broken through into our dimension or vice versa. The significance of this is not yet known but you can be sure that just like everything else we have experienced there is something of importance about it. Everything happens for a reason and that reason can be a whole journey of discovery.

DOWSERS.

There are also negative energies and mischievous spirits out there that will try and play tricks with you but if they are not of Love and Light then they won't hang around for long when challenged. Many negative energies are lost souls or souls still hanging around on the Earth plane. Some just want help in finding the light and passing over.

We are all souls within a Human form and our physical bodies are vessels in which to experience life on this Earth plane. When we pass we have the choice to stay and linger or to go to the light. Many stay sometimes because they are fearful of what they are going to. Some don't realise that they have passed on due to a sudden death and some wish to stay close to the physical realm for a number of reasons.

A great number do however want to go to the light and it is those souls that are sometimes in need of direction and we have on many occasions fulfilled this role with our dowsers or pendulums. After finding lost souls attached to our own energy fields we act as a signpost, pointing these souls in the right direction.

We firstly ask for the necessary guidance and protection from Archangel Michael, who is also the Archangel who takes souls into the light. Then we create a vortex for which these souls can enter through in order to get to the light. We ask Michael to collect these souls and escort them safely to the other side, where very often their family members and loved ones are waiting to be reunited with them. We seal the vortex and thank all involved.

We can sense when a spirit has attached itself to us as we begin to feel sluggish and out of sorts. This is often because these spirits will feed off your energy to use for themselves in order to keep energised. We feel instantly better once they have passed on and left our energy fields.

Dowsers are useful tools when used correctly, and as you are speaking to your Higher Self and Guides you are safe in the knowledge that the information that it gives you is for your highest good and is of the truth.

ASCENDED MASTERS MOTHER KWAN YIN AND MOTHER MARY.

As previously mentioned we have had divine contact with a number of Ascended Masters but the most memorable occasions occurred during the space between sleep and wakefulness. Sarah recalls two of these divine visits in her own words:

"One morning at 4am in March 2009, whilst in an in between state, not asleep but not fully conscious I suddenly began to smell a beautiful aroma which I would describe as Oriental. My ears began to buzz very loudly, with different pitched tones high & low as if being tuned into a Radio channel.

I was aware then that there was a presence stood next to me where I was sleeping. I was aware that this presence was trying to speak to me due to the tonal noises taking place.

I immediately and telepathically said "If you are of the Love and Light then you may stay". My ears began to buzz as if in response to my request. I asked telepathically who I was speaking to and all the time the name Kwan Yin kept coming to mind. My eyes were open when I was asking questions and I could see a haze standing next to me which felt like a loving presence that made me feel at ease.

Each time there was an answer to my questions I would close my eyes to allow telepathic communication to flow, although there seemed to be some tuning problems on my part which made communication difficult. I was aware that the presence who I believe was ascended master Kwan Yin, was about to leave, and shortly before departing the words "I am in spirit form" flowed neatly into my brain.

The presence then disappeared. I was amazed. I hadn't telepathically communicated with anyone that I was aware of before but this just seemed so easy and natural once it got going! Sure, there were a few tuning issues to begin with but once they had been addressed, although short, the words spoken were fluent and easy.

It didn't stop there! Two nights later I was to receive another visit from another divine ascended feminine being. This beautiful archangelic presence is better known to us as Mother Mary.

On this occasion, around 03:30am I was asleep. I began to dream about myself and Mick and a friend of ours amongst others. I was aware I was dreaming and during this dream we were at our house which looked a cross between how it really is and the Cottage Healing Centre where we spend a lot of our time. We called a lady from the yellow pages to do some energy work with us at the house. This lady attended straight away and took us upstairs into what was my old bedroom where I grew up. The lady, myself, friend and the other who I can't remember, sat on the bed. They all started to link hands. I took hold of the ladies hand and it felt like an electric current was being sent through my body. The next part was baffling. I started to black out in the dream but in reality, I was aware I was going somewhere. I could see the concerned faces of those on the bed as I started to lose consciousness. I knew then I had gone to another dimension and I guessed that my soul had transcended my dream state. I was in a black room and my stomach was in pain. I was actually about 4 or 5 weeks pregnant at the time in real life and so I felt something was happening in relation to this. Then a beautiful being appeared in front of me, arms outstretched palms facing up to the heavens. In her typical pose, stood in front of me was Mother Mary, wearing a blue and white gown. She was exactly as I had seen her in all the religious pictures. All the time she kept repeating to me "These twins are part of the grand divine plan, these twins are part of the grand divine plan". Still in pain, I felt reassured by what she was saying. It seemed the more I screamed, the less pain I was in so I kept screaming! Eventually, I knew this event was coming to its end. Mary started to fade away and I took one last massive gasp of air and yelled out to ease the pain, transitioning smoothly and then painlessly back into the dream where I had left off.

The lady doing the energy healing, excitedly said to me "Do you realise what just happened". I, still a little in shock and dazed said "What, what am I having"? referring to the pregnancy. The lady replied "Twins, a boy and a girl, how perfect". We laughed and hugged. Everyone then left including the lady who I felt like I knew, or was somehow going to know.

I awoke back into full consciousness, sweating and in amazement at what had taken place, aware that this was no ordinary 'dream'. The power of Mother Mary's presence was so prominent, truly a powerfully divine being.

I woke Mick and told him what had happened and we discussed the possible meanings behind the experience. We were none the wiser. Naturally we assumed that maybe we were to have twins that were part of a bigger picture, but in reality, we are all part of that bigger picture and all have our roles to play in the grand scheme of things. So what else could it have meant?

One thing we did learn in the days to follow was that Kwan Yin and Mother Mary are the Eastern and Western aspects of each other. They are the Yin and Yang of nurturing motherhood and are depicted this way by their relevant cultures, Eastern and Western. Both are ascended masters and both elected to stay close to the Earth to help serve and enlighten humanity today and assist us with our own ascension and spiritual path.

Unfortunately a month or so later, I was to have a miscarriage before ever knowing what this message meant or whether or not there were in fact twins. What we do know is that since this, we have had the spirit of a little girl around us who we both know as 'Josie'. Josie was the name we had chosen for our child had she been a girl. We had both had almost exactly the same visions of this little beauty and what we had been seeing fitted the description of what had been described to us by spiritually aware friends. In our hearts we know that Josie had never really left us but we also know that she will be coming to us again in the future when the time is right.

We still ponder over what the words of beloved Mother Mary could have meant and why the pregnancy didn't work out at that time. An interesting explanation came from our friend Richard the Angelman. In that, it is possible that the twin aspect of the pregnancy could have been the twin flame or soul mate of Josie and for one reason or another the other part of the duo didn't or couldn't work out, which meant that the plan was put on hold. At least for now...

Another interesting story we came across was that of a similar experience of a woman in Australia some years ago. She had a miscarriage which she was later told in a clairvoyant reading was due to the need for a live energy inside her. This was to open her up to be able to channel her own spirit guides and other light beings and that the soul of that child was working with her from the other side as a guide.

As I said, we now know that Josie is with us and I know that she is working with us from the other side. But as for the reason for all of this...? Well, as we know, there is always a reason. It was hurtful at the time but we know that we are here to learn lessons, some being painful ones. Ultimately we grow stronger from these experiences and the old adage "What doesn't kill you..." applies!

CHAPTER 6: AN OUT OF BODY EXPERIENCE & THE COTTAGE STAY OVER

The experiences we have outlined in this book so far, some if not most people would describe as strange at the very least. We understand! We didn't ask for any of this stuff to happen to us and looking back over the experiences we can hardly believe it ourselves! However, these events to us are not strange, they are absolutely stunningly beautiful. One thing is for sure though, we don't just believe anymore... we KNOW! Know that life is so beautiful and precious but that there is so much more to it if people would only allow themselves to see it. Just let it in and watch your whole life transform for the better and add to your human portfolio of experience an array of spectacular events.

For example, ever wondered what it would be like if your soul self could actually leave your physical body without dying? Well it is a very real possibility and one that Sarah has since come to experience for herself. The difference with an out of body experience and dying is that when you die, your life cord is severed, disconnecting you from the physical body and preventing you from re-entering it. Have you literally died? In the physical sense – yes. In the sense of our true reality? Far from it! In fact it is impossible for us to actually die. Remember, we are *Spirit*-ual beings having a human experience. When we have fulfilled our time here in the physical we depart back into the true sense of our self, back into the infinite soul consciousness that we are. We simply move onto the next experience, be that coming back to the Earth plane for a different experience, going off to another planet to take a well earned rest or simply floating around in the Heavens for a time! Anything is possible.

Following the physical death experience, the soul once ready to move on goes through a series of stages or levels on other planes. These planes help the soul to be cleansed and rehabilitated allowing them to move fully into the light and onto the 'other side' as we know it. We as human beings can experience all of these beautiful planes of existence without dying and there are many that practice this today as did our ancestors in lifetimes past. Just think of the Native

American Indian tribes, a deeply spiritual people. They were and still are very in touch with their higher selves, their true infinite selves and practice leaving their physical bodies. It is a case of discipline and mastery of the self and being aware that we are a spiritual being living a physical life. Each of us leaves our body every night when we are asleep. Our soul goes off and can be involved in a number of different activities, often reaching as far as other planets, galaxies and even universes. Many are able to consciously do this though also.

If anyone suffers with sleep paralysis, it may interest you to know that it is mostly caused by the soul or consciousness suddenly leaving the body or just returning to it. The physical body is actually asleep but the sub conscious is fully awake, hence the feeling of not being able to move or make a sound. This can be a terrifying experience as Sarah well knows before she discovered what was actually happening. It seems the more a person struggles against this paralysis, which is the natural thing to do, the worse and more frightening it becomes. However, if you were to relax and stay calm and collected, you will most likely find that you will easily be able to leave your body at this time.

The experience of leaving the body, known as an 'out of body experience' or 'astral projection' is something that I am yet to experience, at least consciously. With astral projection, you enter into a plane whereby you can literally manifest something with a single thought. For example, when in the astral plane, you could think of being on an exotic island far far away and in a split second, you would be there. Or if you wish to be able to fly, you would be able to. Anything is possible and we are not affected by linear time and space. You could even go backwards in time if you wanted to. As mentioned, those that are able to practice this keep themselves disciplined when doing so and take great care when on the astral planes.

Sarah's first conscious experience of leaving her body happened at the Cottage Healing Centre sleep over. For a long time there had been talk of staying over in the 15th Century Building which is steeped in history. With that history comes the remnants of past energies and the spirit from back in the day still lingers. It was often wondered how these inhabitants would take to having people sleep at the cottage overnight with the inevitable noise and disruption that would bring.

However one night in May 2009 thirteen of us would be brave enough to try! Sarah and I were two of the braves. We were not expecting to stay over and had not brought any sleeping equipment with us but we made do with what we had. This was following a celebratory party for the opening of the new cottage shop, also part of the same building. It was a very interesting evening all round!

Shortly after the party had died down we retired inside the cottage where we continued to talk and laugh. Within minutes of our retirement some of us had heard a banging noise coming from the attic area upstairs. Naturally, there were those of us who just had to investigate this disturbance, including Sarah and myself! Three or four of us made our way up the winding and creaky staircase onto the next floor, arriving at the attic door. The door itself is an old style wooden door with a small metal latch to keep it shut. We opened the door and went slowly up the attic staircase where we stood in the attic area.

We could all sense an energetic presence within the attic although no one could actually see anything. We were cold and tingly and there was a pungent smell around. One of the group took several photographs of the area on his mobile phone knowing that quite frequently orbs are picked up on screen. Although with the naked eye nothing could be seen, minutes later when we looked at the photos a number of white orbs could clearly be seen which confirmed that there was indeed a visitor. Having respect for the character, who some at the cottage believe to be Bonny Prince Charlie, we left the attic and visited some of the other rooms. The Cottage Healing Centre in its earlier days used to be a place that Bonny Prince Charlie visited regularly and would stay over on many occasions.

A number of different energies could also be sensed in the other rooms and again when pictures were taken, a number of orbs confirmed this. With this, we returned downstairs and continued with our evening discussing the events so far.

After the excitement had calmed down and after hours and hours of laughter and party spirit, we all chose a floor space to serve as our sleeping area! All of us had a particular area we were drawn to. Sarah and I lay on the floor right next to the entrance door. We both have strong blue protective energies and I personally always feel that I need to be by the door as a sort of guardian. I am told that I have the embodied energy of Archangel Michael which could explain this protective nature.

The night soon turned into the early hours of the morning, 4 am to be exact and still there were those that were fully awake and enjoying the moment. Sleep was on and off in between each fit of laughter amongst the group, particularly those who had elected to sleep upstairs, not mentioning any names!

We didn't really know what to expect but had a feeling some sort of event would take place in view of our location. Well, I can report that we definitely had some experiences! All out of this world... literally! Whilst in and out of sleep I could feel someone or something walking around me. It felt small and childlike or elemental with a teasing sense of humour. I found myself waking up laughing as if I had been told a joke in my sleep, but I couldn't remember what! This continued throughout the few hours sleep I managed to grab.

Sarah on the other hand had a totally different kind of experience. She told me how she had been sleeping when she suddenly sat up as if awake which isn't unusual. Except when you are looking down at your body, which is still lying horizontally and sleeping that is!

Here is the event in Sarah's own words:

" I have been getting sleep paralysis since the age of thirteen but never really understood it. All I knew was that it was terrifying waking up and not being able to move or shout for help. I hadn't had it in a few months but on this night it was to make an appearance. This occasion was totally different however. I was lying on the floor on my right side facing Mick who was asleep on his back. All of a sudden I woke up with sleep paralysis. 'Oh no' I thought, 'Not again'! But for some reason, despite my thinking, I didn't actually feel the need to panic as much, which was unusual. So I tried to bring myself round, trying eagerly to get my fingers and toes moving. Nothing. I tried moving my body. Nothing. All of a sudden, the next thing I know I began reaching upwards and outwards with my arms trying to pull myself up. Brilliant. I'd done it. I was now sitting up on the floor able to move. But that's not it. When I looked round towards Mick, I was still lying there in the same position, fast asleep!

Some how I had popped myself out of my physical body and was now my non physical self. I couldn't believe it. I leaned over to Mick, putting my face right up close with his and was calling his name and rubbing his cheek trying to get him to wake up so he could help. He didn't even flinch. All of a sudden I felt a kind of suction and I was being pulled back into my physical body. I sort of fell back in side ways, right into the position my body was lying in. I could now move again and it was like it had never happened!

What an amazing experience. I never doubted for a second that there is more to us than the physical and I know for definite that death is not the end. Far from it. There is so much more out there for us that we are all a part of and I know now that we are all Spiritual beings having a Human experience.

So this night was a fascinating but bizarre stay. I managed to get myself back to sleep where nothing more could possibly happen as it was getting on for early morning time. Or could it? Well it certainly did. At around 6am I was awoken from my sleep by exceptionally loud banging. I knew immediately that this was coming from the attic, which was the next floor up from where we were. I lay there and listened as the banging continued three or four times. It sounded to me like someone was using all their might to kick the door down. The weird thing is that Mick didn't hear this. For some unknown reason I didn't feel I needed to go and check what was going on. And I didn't hear anyone else get up to check either.

The next morning when everyone was awake it was established that only a few of us had heard the banging. This in itself struck those of us that had heard it as being strange as there were people sleeping in the room next to and opposite the attic who didn't hear it. One of the group that had stayed and heard the banging was clairvoyant and had shortly afterwards interacted with who we now know was a restless spirit.

It is still unclear why some of the group heard the banging and others didn't but it may be a case that the clairaudient abilities of those that did, were tuned in to the correct frequency at this time. Or it could have been that some were on the same dimension at this time. It was interesting whatever the reason and we all have a great respect for this spirit.

Having shared my out of body experience with some people in the group one advised me to look into what is known as astral projection, as a way to help me understand what had taken place. This I did".

Both Sarah and I have had some truly wonderful experiences since the stay over, but it didn't stop there. Still at the Cottage and on the morning after, we all congregated in the main seating area discussing the night's events. There was still an energy running around the room, which I believe was the one I had felt in the early hours of that morning. Two members of the group could actually see it and said it was an elemental, possibly a gnome who was around 3 feet tall. We could see doors being opened quite apparently being pushed, it was brilliant. It is wonderful knowing that we can all interact with these beloved beings and that we can all learn a thing or two from each other. Nothing is separate and we are all part of the same universe and consciousness. This is what we are striving towards today, oneness in all things.

We eventually but reluctantly left the Cottage and went home but I'm sure that we will do it again soon!

ASTRAL PROJECTION - A definition.

Astral projection (or astral travel) refers to episodes of out of body experiences considered to involve an astral counterpart that separates from the physical body and travels to one or more astral planes or the physical world.

Astral projection is experienced as being 'out of the body'. Unlike dreaming or near death experiences astral projection may be practiced deliberately.

Descriptions of such experiences are found in major religious and accounts of the afterlife with the soul's travels being described in such terms as 'an...Out-of-body experience' where the spiritual traveller leaves the physical body and travels with his/her spirit body (or astral body) into 'other' realms.

Since Sarah's experience she has left her body on two other occasions that she has been fully aware of as she describes below:

"Following my experience at the sleep over, I became very interested in the subject of astral projection. I read through as much material on the subject as I could to get a better understanding of it. All of these years I had been panicking about sleep paralysis, not knowing what it was or why it would occur so frequently. I was so relieved to have the answer. Now when I feel it coming on I ask Archangel Michael to be with me for protection and I just go with it. It is an amazing feeling.

I couldn't wait for the next episode and when I felt it starting to happen I couldn't wait to get out! It happened a couple of weeks after the sleep over. We had been out most of the day and when we got home I went upstairs for a nap. I felt so relaxed and could feel myself going into a deep sleep. It was getting on for 9pm when I suddenly felt my body going numb. I started to lose control of my muscles and felt very heavy. Things started to look different. Eventually I couldn't move at all. I told myself 'this is it, stay calm and go with it'. I was now in a position to consciously exit my body.

I started trying to reach out with my arms. Not my physical arms but my spiritual ones! It was such a struggle. I did the same with my legs but didn't seem to be getting anywhere. If anyone could have actually seen my soul trying to leave my body, it would have been hilarious! I was thrashing around, trying to twist and turn, fighting to get out of my physical embodiment! All of a sudden, I rolled over to my left and fell off the bed! Not knowing if that was my body or my soul, I knelt up and looked back at the bed. I couldn't believe it. There was my physical body, sound asleep! I'd made it, I was now on the astral plane.

Beings as this was my first proper experience out of the body I decided to take it slow. The room looked the same but slightly darker. I'd read that when in the astral body you can pass through solid objects like doors and walls for example. I'll give it a go I thought. I headed straight for the bedroom door. Thump! Okay, that wasn't supposed to happen. I walked into the door face first. 'I thought I could walk through things' I said to myself. I proceeded to open the door in the usual way and walked out onto the landing. I was in the same house but things seemed somehow different. I went into the bathroom and looked around before deciding to go downstairs to see Mick. I started to walk down our spiral staircase and when I got half way down I decided I was going to fly. I just felt within me that I knew how to do this so I simply leaned forward from the step and began floating towards Mick, who was sat on the sofa a short distance away. I know it sounds crazy, but I was actually flying! I slowly let myself drift towards Mick who didn't seem to notice me. I got close enough to him and placed my hand on his left cheek and said "Hello darling". Mick suddenly turned to look at me and smiled lovingly. This confused me as I thought I was invisible to him. So I set myself down on the ground and began to panic, taking deep breaths. Mick was still smiling at me. The next thing I knew I was suddenly being suctioned back upstairs and in a flash I felt myself land back in my body with a thud!

I opened my eyes and sat up on the bed. I chuckled to myself realising what had just taken place. How fantastic. I'd done it. I'd consciously left my body fully for the first time and made it back in one piece. Later I asked Mick if he noticed anything unusual at around 9pm. He said he couldn't remember anything but he had been in and out of sleep whilst sitting on the sofa. I explained to him what I'd experienced and noticed a puzzled look appear upon his face when I told him that during the out of body experience I touched his face and said to him "Hello darling". Mick said that was strange because he could vaguely remember something about me touching his face and saying "hello darling". This was very unusual and we discussed how this could have happened.

We came to the conclusion that whilst I was out of body and he was sleeping we must have come into contact on the astral plane, only I had consciously left my body and he not so consciously had done the same.

On another occasion I experienced this astral projection Mick and I had just arrived home from a weekend in Wiltshire having been crop circle hunting! We plonked ourselves on the sofa and switched on the tv. Within half an hour I had fallen asleep. Again I felt sleep paralysis taking over my body and again I relaxed and let it be. I began trying to squeeze out of my body with my arms reaching out as if to lever me forwards. I suddenly found myself upstairs in the bedroom. I lay on the bed and sang to myself for a few minutes. I then stood up and went back downstairs and sat back on the sofa, watching the tv. Mick was awake and was still also watching the television. I felt him gently move to one side and then I woke up. I sat up in confusion, thinking I had already been awake. I realised then I had been out of my body wondering around the house and had eventually sat back on the sofa to watch tv. All the time my body had been asleep but my soul had been having a wonder around the house! I told Mick what had happened to me this time and he laughed in amazement. It seems I am quite comical when out of or trying to get out of my own body!

There have been a couple more occasions that I have since felt myself starting to exit my body or just returning to it but so far I have not had the chance to experience the astral plane to its full potential when consciously aware. I have no doubt though that with a bit of self discipline and mastery I will be able to control exactly what happens when I am practising astral projection".

CHAPTER 7: CLOSE ENCOUNTERS

Following our amazing experiences we began to awaken to all manner of weird and wonderful things. We had seen UFO's on a number of occasions before our experiences but we began seeing them on a regular basis and went from a state of unknowing to encyclopaedic knowledge in a relatively short space of time.

We looked deeply into this subject and realised that everything spiritual, cosmic and angelic is all connected in a sense of 'Oneness' and divinity. Nothing is bound or restricted to any particular religion and it is accessible to all of mankind. We soon realised that we categorised everything into separate boxes. For example, in our eyes, UFO's were UFO's, aliens were aliens, ghosts were ghosts and angels were angels and so forth. The amazing thing is we now know this is not the case.

Everything is 'One'. We are all connected in more ways than many of us care to realise. Many still see 'aliens' as being little green men. We know that this is just one part of the cosmic canvas and there are many more 'beings' in existence. Many are very similar to ourselves and have reached a higher level of spiritual consciousness. Their knowledge of universal laws, for example the law of physics far exceeds our own understanding hence the sightings of many phenomenal craft in our skies. These kinds of amazing feats are actually available to us but it is a science that we are yet to discover and in turn master.

All of our sightings were documented and sometimes photographed when we were fortunate enough to have our mobile phones to hand to take photographs. Here are some of the sightings that were recorded and documented:

March 2007 Rome Sighting.

While most of the incidents took place in the Birmingham area of the Uk, the first significant sighting that Sarah and I saw together took place on the 31st March 2007 while we were on holiday in Rome.

It was 6.30pm and we were both out walking the streets of Rome after a day of sightseeing. We were around the area of the coliseum crossing a small open grassy area between the rows of buildings. Dusk had just started to set in. As we walked, Sarah was looking into the distance over the buildings. I could see her attention had been drawn towards something in the sky.

She could see a light grey oval shaped 'cloud' in the distance that was moving slowly to the left along with the other clouds. This particular 'cloud' stood out as it looked slightly darker and more rounded than all the others.

It looked about the same height as an aeroplane would fly although and seemed to be at least a couple of miles away. Due to the distance it must have been much larger than a plane.

Sarah watched it for several seconds when suddenly it changed direction and started to move back to the right, in direct contradiction to the other clouds! Sarah realised at this point that whatever she was looking at was not a cloud but something else entirely. By this point she had stopped and was staring at the object. She pointed it out to me.

I could now see as the object changed shape to resemble a tornado and it appeared to be spinning and waving from left to right in the sky. Less than a minute later it changed its shape again and became almost spherical, darkening in colour as if seemingly becoming more solid. It then became stationary in the sky!

Sarah decided at this point to get her mobile phone out and started to video the object.

While watching the anomaly, it began to fade inwards and outwards. We couldn't tell whether this was due to it moving closer or if it was becoming more solid in nature. It did this for about thirty seconds and then without warning, split into two separate smaller circular shaped objects. These began to move around each other, darting about the sky in curved patterns. It was apparent that the objects certainly seemed controlled in some way.

Thirty to forty seconds later the objects moved together and formed one object again! After this, it split once more into two and then became whole a second time. It eventually started to fade away from our sight until it had vanished completely.

Other people in the area at the time didn't seem to notice the object at all, certainly not those within our vicinity.

This was the first unusual event that I had ever seen so I was excited to discuss it with Sarah and our family. Whatever it was, it managed to both stop still in the air and go against the wind direction and manoeuvres that the smaller spherical shaped objects performed seemed far from what we know as natural. It had completely defied the law of physics. The fact that it formed numerous different shapes makes it improbable that it was some sort of floating object such as a balloon.

Our drawing showing the different shapes that the object formed:

age

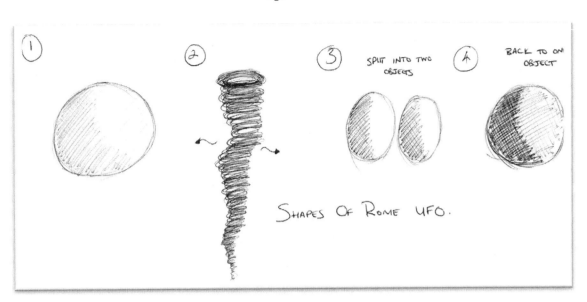

June 2007 Staffordshire Sighting

This incident took place on a hot clear summer's day. It was about 1.00pm in the afternoon and both Sarah and I were out on the road driving in our car.

We were in the town centre not far from home and just approaching Tamworth snow dome. There are two islands close to the snow dome, and it is between these that the sighting took place.

As we went round the first island Sarah suddenly noticed two objects in the sky off to our left out of the passenger seat window.

Initially I couldn't see these crafts, being the driver of our vehicle but as we continued along the road towards the second island it was then that I managed to get a visual of them.

There were two metallic grey cigar shaped objects, one positioned above and to the right of the other. They were smooth and had no visible markings on them and they were quite low in the sky and seemed to be very large. They appeared to be the size of a standard airliner. These objects were stationary in the sky and less than a mile away from us.

We spotted a third object which appeared the same as the others over to our right hand side. It was the same height in the sky as the other two. We began to head around the second island and when arriving on the other side the objects had suddenly all completely vanished. We didn't see them disappear. We just looked and couldn't see them any more.

From start to finish the whole sighting only lasted around ten seconds and no-one else appeared to see the objects.

This is how the first two objects appeared and looked.

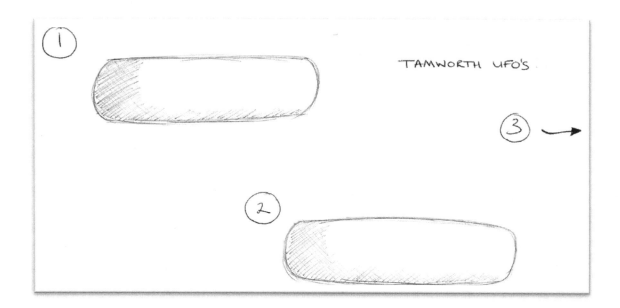

August 2007 West Midlands Sighting.

This incident occurred in August 2007. It was 10:30pm and both Sarah and I were out on a night duty in the area of Birmingham but in separate locations.

It was a beautiful glistening night. The air was still and the sky was covered with a blanket of twinkling stars. I was standing on the street with a colleague when suddenly we noticed what looked like a bright orange orb of light in the sky some distance above us. I estimated that it was about two hundred feet high and was less than one mile away. It was moving slightly faster than an aeroplane but the size of the object was difficult to judge. It seemed about the size of a small aircraft.

At first due to its brightness we thought it was a plane in distress possibly with an engine fire. We stared at the object and watched as it moved across the sky in front of us. It seemed to be moving in a circular path heading away from us so by the time it was on our left it was quite a bit further than it had been when we first spotted it. Eventually we lost sight of the object which we attributed to the distance. It had taken a couple of minutes to make this manoeuvre. There were several other professional witnesses to this sighting all in agreement that it was unusual.

I called Sarah to let her know about this mysterious object and she made her way over to the exact area a short time later. My colleague and I left the area moving on to another of the night shifts surprises, the object having disappeared.

Sarah called me minutes later excitedly explaining to me that the object had reappeared and was in almost exactly the same position I had described to her earlier. It had come around again for a second circuit and took almost the same route as before until it once again disappeared. It was as if the orb had returned for a second look at us Earthlings!

This was to be the last time we saw the object on this occasion.

Sketch by Sarah showing the area, her position, and the object:

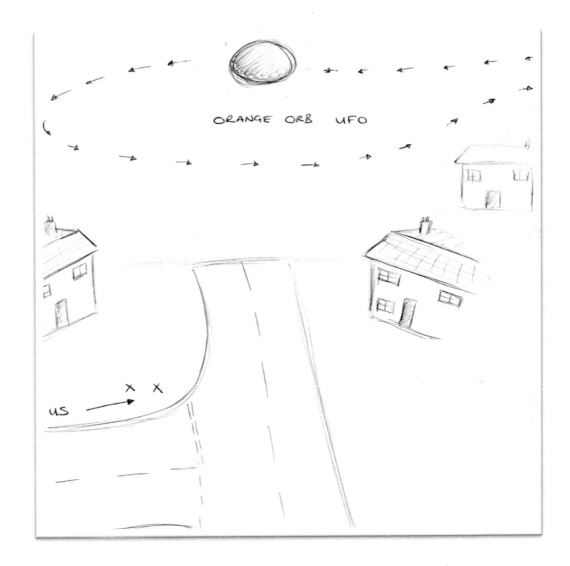

This was not a Chinese lantern! These tend to drift randomly and do not fly on a direct path, especially not twice in a row. Nor was it a plane, helicopter or meteorite. So what was it?

This photograph taken by Sarah is interesting. This is the original with a close up enhancement of the object:

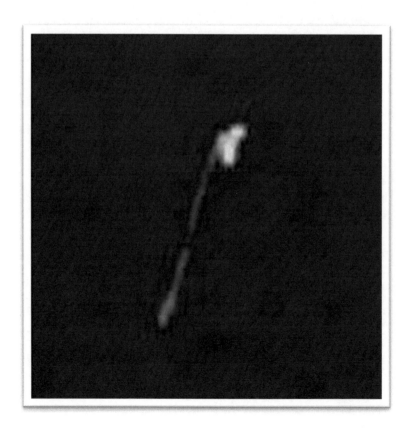

The most unusual thing about the photograph is that it captured a different shape to what we actually saw with our eyes. To both Sarah and I the object looked like a clear round orange orb of light, like a blazing fire. However on the photograph it appears to be a roughly rounded shape with a long hanging 'tail' coming from underneath it. The photograph was not prolonged exposure so it is not caused by the objects movement.

May 2008 West Midlands Sighting

When this bizarre sighting took place Sarah and I were on a night duty together. It was getting on for midnight and was a clear night with the stars visible in the sky.

We were travelling along Chester Road North. The day time traffic had died right down and the road was quiet. On the approach to a large island we both suddenly saw a very unusual object in the sky straight ahead of us.

This object was a glowing light blue coloured tear drop shaped solid object and literally appeared in the sky. The object looked about 200 feet high and was less than a mile away from us. It was moving very slowly in a diagonal path towards the ground. We watched it for about five seconds when suddenly the object came to a halt in the sky, retaining its shape.

A couple of seconds later it started to flicker almost like a candle. Then a small spherical shaped object detached itself from the front of the tear drop craft. It was the same colour and seemed to be breaking away from the main object. Suddenly both objects flickered together before vanishing without trace. We were completely baffled by what we had just witnessed.

A friend of ours told us about a similar object he had seen previously not too far away but what he saw he believed had actually Landed! It sounds crazy I know but what Sarah and I had seen on this occasion, was actually not too far above a local municipal park and before it vanished, for a second we thought it would continue into the park!

Sarah's drawing of object/objects seen:

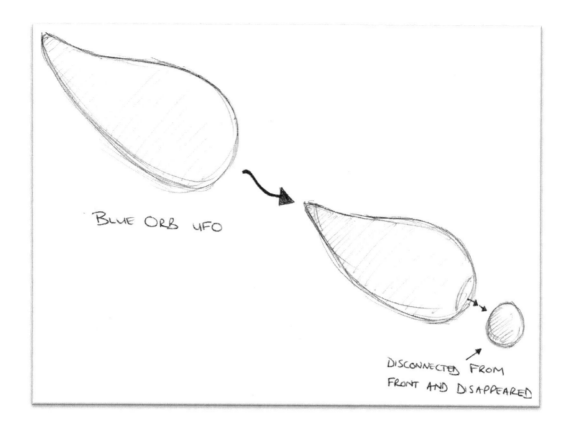

June 2008, More West Midlands Sightings

The unusual series of incidents that took place in the early hours of June 11th 2008 covered numerous areas of the Birmingham area. It is not known whether or not all these incidents were related, however there seemed to be too much going on for it to be coincidence alone. To this day it has never been adequately explained.

Sarah and I were out at night in the Great Barr area of Birmingham. We had a call on our radio asking us to investigate an alarm at a local sports centre that was going off.

We arrived at the centre around 1am in the morning. It was a clear night with very little cloud cover and the stars were visible. We parked up the car outside the gate and got out but soon found that we could not get past the security gates. As we waited and talked, Sarah looked up into the night sky and saw a white light, similar to a star but brighter.

It was moving quite fast across the sky, far too quickly to be a plane. It looked like it was very high up, about 35000 feet, and was pulsating with light very slowly. We watched it for about 8 seconds until it disappeared into the distance. Seconds later Sarah saw a stationary white light appear, then vanish and reappear a short distance away from where it had first been.

This light was stationary at first, then it began to slowly move away from us, pulsating in the same way that the other object had done. A few seconds later I looked to the left and saw what looked like a shooting star speed across the sky. But then moments later a second shooting star took exactly the same path as the first had! We were puzzled by this. It seemed very odd that two would do exactly the same thing in quick succession.

Just after the shooting stars appeared we were radioed and informed that there had been a massive power cut in two large areas of Kingstanding and Sutton Coldfield.

Soon afterwards, numerous residents called in from completely different areas all reporting the same thing, their house alarm was going off and they could see a shadowy figure or figures moving around in their rear gardens. They could never give a good description, just that there was something moving around. Various officers including myself and Sarah were sent out to investigate these reports, but were never able to find any explanation behind them.

One officer was ordered to return multiple times to the same property. He checked it out and there was no-one there, but then minutes later the resident called back to say there was movement outside again.

It felt really bizarre that at least five people from different areas of Birmingham would individually report the same thing at the same time. Sarah and I were called out to an estate in Erdington close to where the other events were occurring.

When we arrived the power was still on, and as we were chatting to a young man about the reported incidents, suddenly everything went dark and alarms started going off. The power had cut out. Moments later we heard a massive explosion from somewhere nearby!

We received a radio call which informed us that the explosion was possibly the sub-station in a few streets away. We drove there to investigate.

We arrived at the sub station and could see nothing wrong, but suddenly there were several underground explosions in the next street, about 500 yards from where the sub station was situated. We watched as a manhole cover got blasted right into the air! Nobody seemed to have an explanation as to what was going on. It was all becoming very bizarre. We felt that we were not in control and the atmosphere was very eerie. After this, things seemed to settle back down and the night shift was nearly over.

In the morning we heard that the electricity board that had attended and repaired the problem underground had said there had been nine incidents in the local area. He said that this was very unusual indeed. Apparently there would usually only be one or two incidents a night but not nine.

We arrived home following the shift and began to use our computer to record some of the night's events. However, the computer had other ideas. It randomly shut itself down and when sending an email about the incident, all of our emails saved, disappeared in front of our eyes. We eventually got the computer on and sent the email however for a time afterwards continued to have computer and internet issues. Our phone also began making automatic calls to people, and would make strange clicking noises upon anyone mentioning the word 'UFO' or similar.

We believe that these events are all linked in some way are and that we were being monitored by government communication head quarters otherwise known as GCHQ, because of what we had and continued to witness.

The electricity board for Birmingham, Central Networks was contacted by a local UFO group and they confirmed that they received complaints reporting power failures in the areas of Kingstanding and Sutton Coldfield, however said they had none on record from Erdington. This does not necessarily mean that there wasn't one, it just means nobody rang the company to complain about it.

They also confirmed that at 12.35am where myself and Sarah were, a faulty cable sparked. This must have been what we witnessed, although the contact at Central Networks was confused as to how this could have looked or sounded like explosions in any way. Despite having them on record, the person spoken to could not give any possible causes for the power cuts, she was just able to confirm that they did take place.

Sarah and I along with others felt that something bigger took place that morning, but we may never know for definite.

October – December 2008 Birmingham Sightings

From October 2008 Sarah and I experienced a huge wave of UFO sightings totalling around thirteen visuals of strange objects in the sky. Many, but not all of these have been similar in shape and form. We feel that part of the reason we see so many UFO's is because we are now more aware of their presence and spent much time looking up at the beautiful sky.

This wave of sightings began late in the evening of October 16th 2008. Sarah's Dad rang her to say that he could see something unusual in the sky over the centre of Birmingham from his back garden. Sarah and I drove over to his house to take a look for ourselves.

Amazingly, the object was still there when we arrived some twenty minutes later. Sarah's Dad pointed the object out to us. Initially, it looked like nothing more than a bright star low down in the sky. For once, we felt as though on this occasion, we were the sane ones! However, Sarah's Dad then told us to check the object's position in relation to a fixed point such as a tree or building top. When we did this we could see that the object was moving very slowly to the West. The rest of the sky remained stationary so the movement was not just due to the rotation of the Earth. We then looked at the object through a pair of binoculars and every time myself and Sarah checked the object, it looked different.

At first it appeared as blue, white and red lights stacked on top of each other. Then the lights had shifted to a different layout. It then looked like two white lights with some sort of black band between them. We knew that what we were looking at was not a plane or helicopter. After a while the object vanished, going out of sight due to the distance it had travelled. This was the first of many occasions that we saw this particular object.

The next phenomenon occurred for Sarah on 28th of October whilst she was in the Sutton Coldfield area. Sarah described seeing a stationary blue light in the sky. As she watched, a smaller red light appeared to one side of it. Then she saw the complete object separate into two bright white lights which moved across the sky descending in a wavy pattern.

What sort of aircraft would be responsible for the lighting patterns and movement witnessed? We have tried to think of all the possibilities but could not come up with any modern day craft that we know of that could move in this way or has such lighting patterns.

In another sighting on November 12th Sarah and I were on our way home after finishing duty.

We saw two glowing white lights hovering in the sky out of the car window. One seemed brighter than the other. Sarah got on the phone to her Dad, who informed her that he was observing an object at home too!

Just then, the dimmer of the two objects we were observing completely vanished into thin air. It was as if someone had switched the lights off! Sarah excitedly told her Dad Kevin about the object disappearing and at precisely the same moment, Kevin informed her that a second object had just appeared next to the one he was currently watching!

It was almost as if one of the objects had teleported and reappeared elsewhere. Was this the case? We don't know. What we do know is that there is no such thing as coincidence.

On the evening of November 17th 2008 Sarah was travelling along a Road in Erdington of the Birmingham area, when In front of her she suddenly noticed two bright white glowing orbs travelling slowly across the sky. There were no stars in the sky at this time as it was at a time where light was only just turning to dark.

Suspecting these objects to be more than met the eye, Sarah pulled her vehicle over and took a photograph of the anomalies on her mobile phone.

Later on, however, when she checked the photograph she found that one of the objects had appeared as a long curved line and the other object to the lower right of the first was barely visible. Yet another object which had appeared different on a photograph than it did from the naked eye.

Below is the photograph taken by Sarah at the time along with an enhanced shot of the object.

Unfortunately I didn't get to see this sighting for myself but I thought that the photograph was amazing!

In the early hours of 19th November 2008 I was in the Sutton Coldfield area on duty with a colleague. We were in the car travelling along Jockey Road when we spotted an orange orb of light in the sky off to the right.

As I drove along the road the object flew straight across my view of the road ahead in a curved path until it settled on my left side of vision. My colleague couldn't believe his eyes and in a state of shock shouted out "What the f***'s that"!! At this moment I could see it had a red tail like structure sticking out from behind it. Seconds later it disappeared in the blink of an eye and without warning.

I was certain that it was not any conventional aircraft. The object seemed too slow for a meteorite and too quick for anything else. It also took on a curved trajectory. Its unusual shape suggests it was not a lantern or balloon of any kind.

Mick's drawing of the object seen on 19th Nov and its movement path.

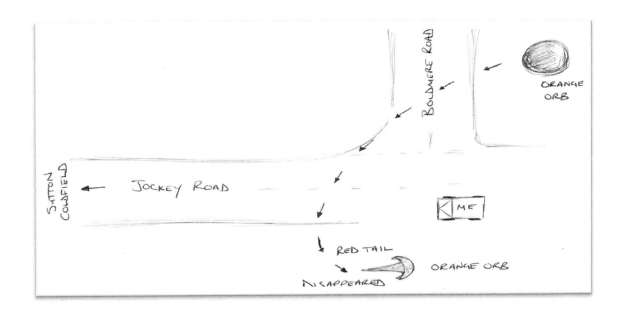

Another of these incidents took place outside our home in Tamworth on 1st December 2008.

It was a dry and clear night with minimal cloud, and very little light pollution from street lights. Sarah and I spotted the first object in the sky at around 11.30pm.

It appeared as a bright orb of light that appeared to be pulsating. The light was mostly white in colour but occasionally other colours were visible within it. The object was moving very slowly from the left to the right of our viewpoint and seemed to be very far away from us. We stood outside the front of our house watching it. Then around fifteen minutes later a solid orange orb of light passed directly over our heads heading in the direction of Polesworth.

We estimated that this orb was travelling around 300 mph and was 2000-3000 feet above us. Two minutes later another orange orb appeared. This one was brighter than the first had been and was slowly pulsating every couple of seconds.

Rather than travel on the same path, this second orb travelled towards the initial white light. It suddenly came to a halt a short distance away from it and remained stationary for around thirty seconds. It almost looked like the two objects were communicating with one another in some way.

Then the orange orb moved off also in a direction towards Polesworth and shortly disappeared seconds later. The white light remained visible, and continued on its slow path across the sky. I tried to take some footage of it on my mobile phone but sadly it didn't turn out as the objects were too far away. Oddly, as I took my phone back inside the house, the voices of the characters of the television programme that was playing in the living room began sounding through my phone as if somehow the frequencies had become entwined. This has never happened before and has not happened since.

In total we observed the initial object for about half an hour, by which time it had moved across the sky in front of us. During this time we spotted numerous other normal aircraft which did not seem to be reacting at all to the presence of the unusual orb like objects. Both Sarah and I feel sure that the objects were something unorthodox.

Another of the many sightings occurred in January 2009 whilst Sarah and I were away in Jersey of The Channel Islands, taking a well earned break! It was a beautiful, clear but cold winter's day with the sun beating down on us. We were walking along the promenade next to the beach when I suddenly noticed a shining object approximately 800 feet above us. I pointed this out to Sarah and we both stood still to look at this object. It was a silver metallic teardrop shaped object and was moving at around 30 – 40 mph across the sky towards the sea. We lost sight of it and continued on our journey, discussing the unusual craft as we went. Minutes later, I spotted the teardrop craft again taking the exact same course as before but going further away from us. We could both see that this was not a plane of any kind and the object was completely silent. This object again disappeared in roughly the same direction as before, this time, not to be seen again.

These sightings are occurring with such regularity that we are no longer surprised when we see them. We know that what we are observing are un-Earthly craft of some kind that are able to perform controlled movements.

These sightings are occurring for a reason and we believe that this is a build up to some sort of major event. This, we will cover in the next chapter.

We feel privileged to have seen so many of these beautiful and wondrous crafts. It is almost as if 'they' are showing themselves on purpose for some reason. We have learned that for those residing upon the higher dimensions, they must slow their own vibratory rate down to a level so as to be seen in our 'physical' world and so as we humans can observe them with our limited visible sight range.

We are all currently going through an evolutionary period, or ascension where our own vibratory rate is increasing, opening us up to all manner of exciting possibilities. Possibilities we once thought impossible or mythical. But think about it, more and more people are witnessing these incredible craft in the skies and the unbelievable movements and feats they display. Are these events merely miraculous, or are they a science we are yet to master?

CHAPTER 8: GALACTIC FEDERATION OF LIGHT

As mentioned in Chapter 7, we have seen many unusual craft in the skies. As a result we have been led to do some research into this subject and looking for answers as to why these sightings seem to be increasing, not only for ourselves but for many all around the world. You only have to pick up a newspaper to see another report of UFO's in the sky, not to mention the endless pictures and video footage now available on the internet. This is all indicative that the phenomenon seems to be reaching new heights of awareness amongst the populations.

During our research not only into this phenomena, but others too, information has practically thrown itself at us! It seems the alarm clocks that we set before incarnating onto the Earth this time round have gone off with a bang! It was time for our awakening and fortunately Sarah and I have been making this journey together. With this awakening came a lot of amazing experiences and reclaimed knowledge. I say reclaimed as since making this journey we realised that much of this knowledge and experience was already inside us. It is a case of reclaiming and allowing this to surface once again so we can move forward in our lives and on our soul journey.

We have discovered that much of what we know leads back to ancient times when other civilizations were present on the Earth. Taking these interstellar crafts for example, did you know that there is actual preserved artwork from cave walls that depict space rockets? Not only that, but alongside these rockets are clearly drawn spacemen wearing space suits with helmets over their heads. This art dates back to the day of the caveman. This would surely have to make any cynic wonder.

What we now know is that since the beginning of time, or what we perceive time to be, we have been visited and watched over from the stars and this interaction between humans and cosmic beings has been ever present.

If we look at the 'Lost' city of Atlantis which some still believe to be a myth, they had technology that far surpasses anything materially that we have today. We feel that we are technologically advanced in today's society but what we have learned is that a lot of the knowledge from days past is suppressed and hidden from us by those that have only their own best interests at heart.

The interaction between Atlanteans and cosmic beings led to such buildings as the great pyramids of Giza in Egypt. These structures, as well as others around the world are strategically placed to correspond with certain star systems. This is also true of ancient monuments such as the stone circles. Ask yourself honestly, how could 'primitive' man build such wonders?

So where is this all going? Well during our journey and experiences with these extraterrestrial crafts we came across an organisation called the Galactic Federation of Light, otherwise known as the Federation of Light or as we like to call them, 'The Fed'!

The Galactic Federation of Light consists of many races of beings from many different planets and have been around for aeons of our time. There are many channels upon the Earth plane that bring the messages of the Galactic Federation of Light to those that are willing to listen.

Their messages are consistent with the information above and they are working closely with us now in order to assist in the raising of the vibrations of the Earth and those that live on her. They are subsequently assisting in the ascension of those that are ready to raise themselves to such a level. Note the word 'assist'. We are a freewill planet and this is greatly respected by those of the light including those of the light that are not of the Earth. It is therefore our choice individually if we wish to participate in our own ascensions and awake to the calling card we set for ourselves. The Federation of Light along with the Angels, Ascended Masters and other beings of love and light will not force anything upon us and can only intervene if given permission by ourselves, unless it is the will of the creator.

We regularly listen to these messages channelled by willing participants of the light and are always astounded at the accuracy of the information being spread in describing the circumstances at the time. Changes that are taking place, feelings that may be being felt along with advice and support are the general theme. The acknowledgement that everything is Love, all is 'One' and nothing is separate from the creator or each other is forefront.

The beings of the Galactic Federation are our brothers and sisters from other places and they are with us at this difficult time on Earth where things seem to be changing by the day. Old structures are breaking down making way for the new with the old negative energies being dispersed and eventually transmuted into light. We are feeling the pinch so to speak as we watch the banks collapse and jobs disappear as well as mal practices being exposed of our governments. This is something that was channelled from the Federation many months before any of it actually occurred. The message was not to be afraid. Although it is a difficult time for a lot of us, what is happening is part of the rebirth of our new world and existence.

Something else we have come to realise is that our souls or our divine sparks of light as we really are may have originated in other parts of the universe. We participate in lifetimes in a certain place in accordance with what we need for our soul's development. One way in which you can find out where your home planet is, is to meditate upon it. Have the intention to go back to your origins and see what comes about. It may take you a while or it may come straight away. Sarah and I participated in a meditation one night in order to find out where we were from. Following the meditation we both came round having received the same thing. The Pleiades! The Pleiades, also known as the seven sisters is a star system visible from the Earth. It is an open star cluster in the constellation of Taurus and is among the nearest star clusters to Earth and is the cluster most obvious to the naked eye in the night sky. Its people are similar to us, most being humanoid in appearance.

The Pleiadians are among those aboard the Federation of Light star ships assisting us in our current Earthly missions. One of the things myself and Sarah have in common is that since a very early age we have both looked to the stars and felt a longing to go 'home'. Having been told that we are from the same place, this explains us having the same vision during our meditation. As previously mentioned in Chapter 4, we recently discovered that we both have a guide named Amanda. We discovered that Amanda is a cosmic being from Sirius, the brightest star we are able to see in the night sky. It is also known colloquially as the 'Dog Star', reflecting its prominence in its constellation, Canis Major. Amanda is also part of the Ashtar Command, a galactic fleet commanded by Ashtar himself and part of the Galactic Federation of Light.

Whilst on the subject of Sirius, some months ago Sarah had a conversation with a cat. Now I understand that this may sound a little odd to some! However, animals are as much a part of the oneness as we humans are and we were all created in the same way and with love. The only difference is their souls chose a different evolutionary path. Back in the days of old, we hadn't lost touch with our ability to communicate with animals as well as other spiritual beings currently considered to be on the other side of the veil. Her conversation went like this:

"I was staring out of the bedroom window away with the fairies and in a world of my own when I suddenly became aware of a cat lying in the grass just outside our house. The cat was looking up at me staring into nothingness and I then felt myself engage with him. Telepathically I asked of the cat "Where are you from"? Referring to home planet. I immediately received into my mind the words "Sirius. What about you"? Feeling a bit bonkers at this point I could see that the cat was still staring straight at me and hadn't taken his eyes off me. I then replied back in my mind, concentrating on the cat "I think the Pleiades as it seems to keep coming up". Still staring at each other intently, the cat then slowly got up and casually stretched his body before strolling off.

As you can imagine, I was very surprised at what had just taken place but was quietly pleased! I know animals can understand us when we speak to them but to know that we can communicate with them on a completely different level that goes beyond the barrier of language and species is a privilege. Little did I realise at the time that Mick was in the next room and could also see the cat looking at me, not taking his eyes from me. He said the cat seemed to be in deep concentration, enough to draw even his own attention".

With regard to the Ashtar Command Sarah also very recently had an interesting encounter which was later confirmed to be Ashtar Command. Here's what she had to say:

"It was 06:20am early in August 2009. I was still in bed just starting to stir. As I was beginning to wake I was aware of a male voice talking to me and had been for a while. I managed to keep hold of a couple of sentences and these are the words I can recall:

"This new world will be one where all giveth, where light covers the dark, where love is the only rule".

I could hardly believe what I had heard but events like this were happening more and more these days so I was becoming comfortable with it. I ran downstairs and grabbed a pen and paper and wrote the words down while I could still remember them, as I didn't plan on staying awake for very long! I took the pen and paper with me and after a quick appointment with the lavatory went back to bed and quickly began falling back to sleep. As I began drifting away, again a voice began to speak to me saying:

"Heaven comes into us all" followed by the vision of a rectangular Yin Yang symbol in my minds eye.

I opened my eyes and checked the time. It was 06:30 and I recorded the words on my piece of paper next to our bed. It didn't take long before I eventually did fall into a deep sleep where there wasn't much chance of anything being able to wake me from then on"!

I had my own experience with The Federation of Light some months before Sarah's experience.

They had left for a short absence at the end of 2008 leaving the channeller and us with the lessons they had brought, allowing us time and space to grow inside. They had not stated when we could expect them to resume communication with this particular channeller, however it turned out to be a few months in duration.

One morning, whilst in the bathroom and without realisation I picked up the sink plug, which incidentally could look like a space ship being silver and disk shaped, and I began to hover this over the plug hole saying to myself "A ship of great size". I then put it down wondering to myself why I had done this.

A ship of great size was how the Federation of Light described one of their vessels to the world in a previous communication. I then went downstairs where I switched on our computer and saw a message that the Federation were back. I had received contact from them telepathically that morning before I had seen any announcement of their return or contact and I was truly amazed. It felt unreal!

The Federation of Light have stated that they are accountable for a large number of UFO sightings in our skies today. They are attempting to gradually accustom humanity to their existence by showing themselves more and more as the truth becomes more apparent. We have been kept in the dark for far too long and great changes are occurring that involve the birthing of our inter-dimensional selves, so that we may live once again as one with all levels of existence. This is the way it was back in the days of Atlantis for example when everything was a part of the whole. The aim is to bridge the gap between Earth and the Universe and to bring Heaven to Earth, working together with our space families!

They have also stated that they are responsible for a large number of crop circles that are appearing around the world. These crop circles, covered in the next chapter, they state are releasing new energies into our atmosphere that are working with us to raise the level of consciousness among us, as well as being messages and communications. Some, they have said are even flags of their nations, and there are some interesting designs coming about!

The Galactic Federation of Light are working closely with us and are very excited of when the time comes about that we can all interact openly with each other. They have announced that they will be making more appearances in the near future especially as we are now on the countdown to 2012.

We look forward to the time of first contact and know it will come about when we are ready for it.

As David Bowie once sang, "There's a star man waiting in the sky..."

CHAPTER 9: CROP CIRCLES

Sarah and I visited some crop circle sites in July 2009. This was a birthday surprise for me organised by Sarah and involved travelling to Wiltshire, UK, where we stayed over and were shown around the sites by a crop circle expert and enthusiast.

I can say that having visited the crop formations that they are definitely not man made and they are truly amazing to see! These formations are of interest to both Sarah and I and I am glad that I have had a chance to see them for myself.

They can only be seen in their true glory from the air. When you are standing inside them on the ground it is impossible to guess the design, even when you know before you enter what the design is. As we stood inside we could both sense a warm energy almost like mild electricity which generated heat inside the actual formations. However, it was a cold and windy day. We later visited and spoke with a well known Professor at his home, near to the crop circle formation sites.

He has spent years and years analysing these circles and studying the sacred geometry associated with them. Like me he acknowledges that they are a communication from intelligent sources which appear to be getting more complex with each one.

So far this season Wiltshire seems to be getting new circles most days, which is amazing considering the size and complexity of them. There is almost no damage to any of the crops, they are bent in all directions but remain intact as if controlled by an energy force, that had respect for the harvest. After a short while, usually within a month, they will raise again and grow towards the sun in order to be harvested. They sometimes appear in a matter of hours, and although night vision cameras of the highest quality cover the area nothing is seen until a crop circle appears visible with the raising of the sun and the break of daylight.

Crop circle of what is believed to be a Mayan Chief

Crop circle depicting 2012 planetary alignment

We now understand that if something's meant to be, then it will be as was the case with my birthday trip. Sarah told me that whilst arranging this birthday event for me that everything just unfolded with ease as she explains here:

"It was around five weeks before Mick's birthday and I had been wondering what I could organise for him. Shortly afterwards we were reading a channelling from the Galactic Federation of Light, on the internet. The channelling was talking about the recent bout of crop formations appearing all over the world, particularly in Wiltshire in the UK. This was one of those light bulb moments where I thought 'Aha'! I knew then what I was going to arrange. A crop circle visit to Wiltshire in one form or another.

I couldn't decide which would be better, a helicopter flight above the formations to appreciate them from the air or a ground trip into the formations themselves. Both would be amazing no doubt. I typed into the internet 'crop circle visits'. I found a site that did ground tours of the formations and were based in the heart of the anomalies in Wiltshire. I then went on to find a site for helicopter flight tours.

I emailed both with my details explaining that this would be a birthday trip and asking if there were any recommended hotels in the area.

I expected to wait a couple of days for a reply from either and so started to look around at accommodation on the internet. I came across a beautiful little country pub hotel next door to 'The Silent Circle', where I had found the crop circle ground tours. This pub was called 'The Whitehorse Inn', namely as it is near to the ancient site of the large chalk white horse located on Milk Hill, near to Alton Barnes. This horse is symbolic of what are known as 'White Riders' who would come and collect any wondering souls from the Earth plane and take them into the light.

To my amazement within a couple of minutes I had received an email back from the ground tour guide of the formations. The date I had requested was available and he would put us in the diary. With regards to accommodation, he said 'The Whitehorse Inn' would be ideal being in the centre of all the action but it would likely be fully booked now due to it being so popular and normally booked up a year in advance. He recommended some other places that would be okay. 'Oh well', I thought. 'I'll give the White Horse a go, you never know'. I emailed the 'Whitehorse Inn' asking availability for the two dates I wanted to book and again to my amazement I had an email back within minutes. This confirmed that those two dates were available. I couldn't believe how smoothly everything was going. I provisionally booked both the crop formation tour guide and the accommodation securing our place. Even the tour guide was surprised at the availability of the 'Whitehorse' saying it was obviously meant to be! It was certainly starting to feel that way.

My ears began ringing which normally happens confirming I have made the right choice. A form of communication from above! I knew there was more to this trip than met the eye. I had been guided to book this particular event for a reason, I just didn't know what that reason was yet!

I didn't receive any email from the helicopter tours until a couple of weeks later and this didn't answer any of my questions. This was a complete indication to me that I had made the right selection!

A week before Mick's birthday I received an email from the tour guide. He said that he had been approached by a BBC television crew who wanted to film him for a documentary on crop formations. This was going to be on the day we were going on our tour and he asked if we minded being part of it. The programme was going to be presented by a famous British actor named Danny Dyer. Naturally I emailed back saying this would be fine and that we were looking forward to it.

Why our day? I couldn't believe how fluently the planning for this day had gone and it definitely felt as if there had been some kind of influence in the organisation of the event. All the pieces were falling seamlessly together without any hiccup, hindrance or problem of any kind!

We both live by the rule 'if it feels right then it probably is'. We know now that we are following our heart which in turn is a form of guidance. This event definitely felt right and we were going to have a fabulous and informative time. As it happens, we got a taster from these formations of Sacred Geometry which whetted our appetite and has inspired us to look into this subject deeper. Maybe one of many reasons why we needed to take part in this event, as well as to have a fantastic time"!

Michael & Sarah at Crop circles In Wiltshire, UK, July 2009

In the background of the picture of Sarah you will see a white horse on the hill. This chalk carved horse is around five thousand years old representing the 'White Riders', a fact that has been known for thousands of years by our ancestors. There are many white horse chalk carvings at many different locations in England. In those days they had a closer understanding of how things are and were not stifled with scepticism. White Riders are indicative that death is most certainly not the end. We have been told by various in tune individuals that we are White Riders and that one of our many purposes is to help souls pass to the other side.

White horse at Milk Hill, Wiltshire, UK

We have also discovered that mysterious geometric shapes have been appearing in crop fields around the world with ever increasing frequency over the last several years also and not just in the UK. With each passing year, these circles and their patterns become more and more complex, depicting ancient symbols, formulas, and even astronomical representations. Inexplicably, it has been known for flocks of birds to break formation whilst flying over a crop circle pattern only to regroup after passing over the anomaly. This may be something to do with the frequencies and energies arising from the formations that birds are aware of.

As always there are critics and sceptics of the phenomenon who state that crop circles are the result of a prank or a hoax, but have yet to explain precisely what method the alleged pranksters would use to produce geometrically perfect designs on the ground. But as I stated previously and having visited the sites and spoken to witnesses I cannot see how any of these crop circles are man made, in fact I guarantee that they are not.

Some of these sceptics, who also doubt the authenticity of the crop circles, have even gone so far as to say that there may be a non-manmade cause for the formations, such as a whirlwind or ball lightning. Because of the inability to adequately explain how they are created, theories about crop circles range from the wonderful to the bizarre.

To state that a whirlwind could account for these complex pieces of art is ludicrous. There is no possible way a whirlwind can cause these crop circles, unless a whirlwind has an understanding of numerology and can communicate with humankind by using sacred geometry that is. In one of the formations there was a clear depiction of our solar system, with each of the planets' positions placed in relation to the Sun as they will appear on December 21, 2012, that date also happens to mark the end of the Mayan calendar.

I believe that cosmic beings are attempting to communicate with mankind. This can be verified by the fact that language has also been used as part of some of these formations that are not of an Earthly origin. They are telling us about mankind, its history and its future of ascension in a beautiful, intelligent and artistic way.

CHAPTER 10: MICHAEL'S MEDITATIONS

When I used to think of meditation, it conjured up the image of a spiritual guru sitting cross legged in a tranquil location, sometimes on a mountain top. Reaching that guru is part of the journey toward self development and fulfilment and once we get there we ask questions about the meaning of life or about how we can attain the perfect life. We often hear that the answers are inside us and that we should go and contemplate.

Well, I am not a wise man on a mountain top and definitely don't have all the answers... Yet! But I'm working on it! I am just like you, living life to the best of my ability and seeking more peace and serenity in my life. I am still learning to do it better, using meditation as a guide, a way of measuring how I'm doing on my journey. Why not take up this journey yourself? Meditation is not difficult and when you can learn to quiet and still your mind you may be surprised at what enters in. Use meditation to find the answers to your questions and allow it to work with your moral compass, the heart.

When we first began to meditate it took some getting used to. We didn't fully understand what it was about or what we were looking to achieve. On the face of it, it seemed simple enough but we discovered that there is more to this than just closing your eyes in a quiet place. We learned that it is important to call in the relevant protection first to ensure that lower forces cannot interfere with this sacred time.

After a few attempts we started to really open up to this aspect of our journey and we began to have amazing visions, words and messages come through to us. Although the meanings are not always clear straight away, in time it all makes sense. We decided to start documenting our meditations and it was only when we began to write them down that the power of these messages came through as they were intended.

We have learned to listen to the messages we receive and also how to interpret them. Our meditations have never failed to intrigue and amaze us. Here I have included some of my own meditations exactly as I recorded them at the time:

1. I said prayer of protection, closed eyes and relaxed.

My right ear began to ring loudly followed by the left, usually signifying a download of information or someone trying to communicate with you. This is often mistaken for tinnitus. The ringing continued.

I saw the image of a tired waiter where we had been for dinner that day. He was rubbing his eyes. I wanted to ask if he was okay but instead I remained in my seat. I heard the words "We are more concerned about our egos and about what people think of us rather than just getting up and helping".

I then felt a dull ache from my heart region which lasted throughout the meditation. I could hear creaking upstairs and so I asked whoever it was to make contact with me. At that point I had the vivid image of a large Angel walking down the staircase to my left. This Angel had a gold shining aura around him. He stood in front of me with his wings fully opened which filled the living room. I then saw the face of Sarah's Guardian Angel before hearing another creek upstairs. The Angel moved his head looking up to the ceiling and said to me "Don't worry yourself about that". I could also sense my own Guardian Angel standing to my right. She appeared frequently during the meditation.

Whenever I ask a question during my meditations I always see the image of old style typewriter keys only these ones are bigger and circular shaped. One has a 'Yes' written on it and the other has 'No' written on it. Sometimes this writing is coloured in bold black and sometimes bold red letters. When I ask my question, one of the keys will raise up prominent in my mind, answering the question as appropriate.

Saw myself standing with lots of money in my right hand and I threw it into the air. I Heard the words "You've got that much you don't need it' in my mind.

2. Our clear quartz crystal was present. Said prayer of protection, closed eyes and relaxed.

There was another noticeable change in frequency in my left ear. I had a flashback of some of my previous meditations. Then saw myself in the clouds and felt I was on horseback, looking to my right towards a male sitting on a white winged horse with armour and sword, turning round and waving his left arm signalling a charge.

Then saw a Hindu/Asian looking belly dancer, dressed in lime green and dancing in the distance but getting closer to my field of vision. I couldn't see her face. I asked who she was and got the name 'Azota' which was said several times and then spelt out several times in my mind's eye. Behind her I could see what looked to be crystal spire shaped buildings, as if like a city.

Then I saw a glass crystal shaped see through object on top of a stick. It was rotating around and I had an image of two hands rubbing the stick which was making the crystal rotate. Later on in meditation I saw the same glass crystal object positioned horizontally and again rotating.

I asked for a vision of my future and was given a picture of a wooden or brown house with me and Sarah and two children, one either side of us and two dogs. We seemed to be posing for a family picture and were either in a field or a large garden connected to the house.

I then saw myself in the Cottage Healing Centre where a friend had given us a card reading whilst sitting on the floor during the sleep over. He said he had just seen something walk past him and as he was saying this I saw the toilet door opening. I suddenly saw an image of Snow White and the seven dwarves and I heard a voice say, 'Only *these* dwarves are real'.

I was now looking at a male in the distance either standing on a hill or something up high. He had a black beard and a moustache and was wearing some sort of gold head piece. I Couldn't make out who it was but the name 'Serapis Bey' came into my mind. He bowed with his palms together toward me and when he got back to the standing position he said 'Namaste'. He waved at me and I came around, out of the meditation. There had been lots of creaking in our house throughout as if beings on the other side of the veil were openly walking around and sharing in this sacred time.

3. This meditation was during an angel class we attended. Said prayer of protection, closed eyes and relaxed. Crystal present.

Guided to enter our clear quartz crystal through the smallest pyramid face. I did so and then saw myself in the middle of a battle whereby I started off on horseback with a sword and was fighting with lots of other people with swords. I jumped off my horse and continued to battle from a standing position on the ground.

I then moved onto another scene where I returned to what I believe was my home somewhere to a female who I sensed was 'Sarah'. The room had marble floors and I was drinking out of a golden chalice which I think had a red ruby on the cup. I believed I was celebrating my return from battle.

I went into another point of meditation and was talking to my Guardian Angel who was saying to me "It's good to be with you again, all will be revealed when the time is right". I thanked her for protecting me and I said "Can you thank your colleague (referring to Sarah's Guardian Angel) for protecting her". She said "I don't need to, he knows you appreciate it". I asked her if her name was Michaela, which I'd come to in a previous meditation. She confirmed that this was correct.

We were then guided by the facilitator to envisage a kind of television screen within the crystal. On that screen I saw a number of flashes. I saw a kind of movie reel of what I believe Atlantean society to be like. Everyone was getting along and were respectful to each other, having a good time and being very laid back. There was no urgency or rush. The people were wearing all in one cotton garments of some kind.

I then came out of the meditation.

4. Clear quartz crystal present. Said prayer of protection, closed eyes and relaxed.

I felt a prickly heat sensation on both my arms which lasted 2 or 3 seconds. I then had the image of Azota, dancing right next to me. It was a small image and she was belly dancing but I couldn't see her face. She was dressed in green.

My Guardian Angel then appeared and flew from right to left. She stopped on my left hand side and was pointing in front of me. As I looked I could see a Middle Eastern type desert city setting. I began to walk towards it. As I got close there was an elderly Arabic looking woman kneeling down. She had gold jewellery coming from her head dress. This was to my left. As she saw me approaching and getting level with her she began to bow down to me. I said to myself "Why is she doing that, who am I". I received no answer.

Next I saw an eagle close to my left eye. It looked at me then turned its head and carried on. I then saw Serapis Bey who was almost level with me. He appeared to be standing on something which was elevating him. He was dressed as before with the same gold head dress.

5. Clear quartz crystal present. Said prayer of protection, closed eyes and relaxed

I could hear a high pitched noise coming from my left ear which lasted for about 5 minutes and then moved to my right ear for the same amount of time.

Had a vision of a young Native American Indian female. This girl was sitting with her back to me and was dressed in Indian attire which was beige in colour with patterns on. She was facing a group of Indian chiefs who were dancing around in a circle. They were very happy and were wearing white feather head dresses.

I could now see a brown eagle flying over me. It did this a few times and then landed on me, gripping my clothing at chest level, its claws hanging onto me. He then flew off.

I suddenly smelt a sweet caramel or toffee aroma which stayed around for a few seconds. I had an image of my Granddad followed by images of other members of my family who have passed, but in picture form. They were coming from both my left and right towards me and then stopped in front of me.

Jesus then appeared. He walked passed me but didn't look to or speak to me. He was collecting lost souls and taking them with him to the other side. Archangel Michael appeared several times holding his sword.

End of meditation.

6. Clear quartz crystal present. Said prayer of protection, closed eyes and relaxed

This was a short meditation but during it I saw an elderly woman pointing at her own mouth and teeth. I couldn't see any features. I suddenly saw fingers making a cutting motion and then gave me the thumbs up! Some of the visions don't always necessarily make sense immediately!

Sarah's Guardian Angel appeared with a large red number 7 behind him. Number seven is often seen as a sign from above that you are on the right path and that the outcome of a situation will exceed your expectations. Sarah had been seeing this number frequently in answer to her prayers in much the same way as the feathers would appear. I had started to see this number too. Images of our Cottage friends appeared and then I once again saw a very brief image of an eagle and even briefer image of Azota.

7. Again with clear quartz crystal. Said prayer of protection, closed eyes and relaxed

This time I was aware of the presence of a female stood in front of me. I couldn't see her face because she was wearing white garments with a hood pulled over. She initially walked in front of me but I knew that she wanted me to follow her. The next thing I knew I was standing next to her holding her right hand. I can remember her being cold to the touch and her skin seemed almost waxy in texture. We were both looking at a light so bright it hurt the eyes. I was looking at what appeared to me to be some sort of craft. There was a male looking down towards me who was humanoid but was tall and had an aura of wisdom about him. At that point I looked to my left and saw a blue orb of energy and I knew immediately to be Archangel Michael. The orb changed to a full size being which was Michael. He said "It's safe, you can go on". I had an overwhelming sense of trust and so I began to walk towards the male. I turned around, Michael had gone but the female was still present. I went onboard this craft and it was really very bright like the inside of a fridge with extremely strong white light. I sat down on a tall pedestal type chair the seat of which was black. I seem to remember seeing two cocktail glasses being brought out on a tray, one containing a blue liquid and the other containing an orange liquid.

I remember having a feeling that there was something missing and I said to the man "Where's Sarah". A voice then said "We'll bring her to you". At that point Sarah came from in front of me being led by a male holding her hand. I couldn't see where she had come from but I sensed she had come out of a room somewhere nearby. Then the voice said "Here's your wife". Sarah was looking at me and smiling and was wearing a white body length cloth type garment which had brown patterns of some sort on the front. She was walking towards me and then the other male just disappeared. Sarah and I were now together again next to each other and my sense of emptiness had gone. I felt complete again.

I was thinking to myself "What time is it"? To which I heard a voice say "Time doesn't mean anything here". I then said "What about my family, are they okay"? The same voice said "Your family are okay, but it's you that needs to be here". I then stood up and walked forwards and could sense the presence of someone else. As I looked around to my right I saw a being who I immediately recognised as Saint Germain. He was dressed in a violet coloured velvet crushed garment. His hands were out in front of him one at the top and one at the bottom and between them he had a Merkaba. He didn't say anything but I got the sense he was implying that I would be learning about the Merkaba when the time was right.

I then remember saying Thank you to everybody and I came back round from the meditation with a 'that's me done for the day' feeling!

CHAPTER 11: SARAH'S MEDITATIONS

Sarah has enjoyed some very interesting meditations. Like me she has had some very vivid experiences and some very touching visions. Sarah acknowledges that not everything in her meditations yet makes sense, but knows that given time all will become clear as it always does. Sarah also says a prayer of protection upon any meditation and calls for the relevant beings of light to be with her during it.

Here are some of Sarah's meditations exactly as she recorded them at the time:

1. The day our clear quartz crystal was ordered. As soon as the 'buy' button was pressed it was as if someone had covered my right ear and my left began ringing loudly for a minute.

I had a vivid vision of old people, suffering on their own or being shipped away to a home. The words "They shouldn't be allowed to live like this" were said. I was then given an image of a beautiful community living in tepees with everyone involved, everyone happy and everyone included and looked after with no need for suffering or loneliness.

Then I had the image of a mouth. It was female with wrinkles around the lips and was talking but I could not hear the words. Next I saw the image of an eagle flying. Then the eagle's head and face was in the centre of my vision.

Felt pressure on my forehead (third eye).

2. The day the crystal arrived.

Saw the Image of the 'Armani' eagle logo. This turned into vision of the eagle flying across my vision. It was then as if I was flying high, looking down over desert like land with a huge river running through it. All of a sudden the face of a beautiful Hindu lady appeared, her face making up the giant moon overlooking the desert. This was in the left hand corner of my vision and she was looking down on this land, eye lids down with a pleasant look on her face and the traditional bindi on her forehead. She was covered by robes around her head. I asked for her name and saw the names Lakshmi, Brahma and Shiva appear in my mind. Maybe I was supposed to work it out for myself!

As I was about to withdraw from the meditation I saw a picture frame with a beautiful picture inside. The picture was of a silhouette with land and a tree to the left hand side and a big beautiful full moon to the left and above the other features.

3. At beginning I started to ask Archangel Michael to help me to discern any information that would come to me during the meditation. I got sidetracked and finished of asking for protection instead! I always start with a prayer of protection and ask for protection from my Guardian Angel also.

I heard the words "You are aware".

I was next given the image of some beggars in Goa (where I had been some years earlier) asking for donations and people just passing by, dismissing them, giving them dirty looks like they were scum. Then the words "And yet we say, if you don't ask, you don't get", were said. I sensed some irony here.

Then heard the words "You don't have to see, you just need to feel". I feel this was because I was trying hard to see visions with my third eye when all I needed to do was relax and let it be.

I became aware of a negative being saying things of a negative nature to me although I cannot remember exactly what. I said to this being "I will only talk to those of love and light so go away please". As soon as I said "please" I became aware of a very strong presence, my Guardian Angel who stepped in and said firmly to me "Don't say please, *tell* them to go away". Felt like I was being told off! I then said to the negative being firmly "Go away"! It went. I felt this situation could have been a test of my discernment. If so, think I'd have scored 7 out of 10 overall!

Heard the words "Adults should be children and children should be adults".

I was aware of a number of people standing around me almost in a semi circle in front of me and one in particular stood out wearing pink garments. I heard the name Babaji mentioned. Babaji is another amazing Ascended Master and it is believed he ascended with his physical body, something we all today have the ability to do.

I kept seeing images of different faces and outlines. One face/outline looked exactly like another well known Ascended Master, Siddhartha Gautama Buddha. This face disappeared and I saw a kind of explosion in my mind, like crystalline. The words "The power of crystal" were said.

I then said "Atlantis" in my mind, wanting to know more about Atlantis. The image of a great stone wall running through Atlantis appeared to me and then heard the words "Wall of Atlantis".

I later looked this up on the internet and found that a structure known as the wall of Atlantis has indeed been discovered.

4. Clear quartz crystal present.

Felt a slight throbbing pain in end of left ring finger and a recurring image of a left hand placed flat down on a table with the end of the ring finger being chopped off!

Again my eagle appeared, this time as if flying in slow motion out of a cloud of smoke towards me. The eagle stopped with its face right in front of my eyes. The eagle appeared a few more times throughout the meditation.

Suddenly had the image of a male body from the neck down, wearing centurion type attire. Bare chested, muscular with a brown strap going across the chest. He was wearing a toga type skirt and had strong legs. On left arm there was a brownish coloured round shield and in the right hand was a spear.

Saw rainbows appear during meditation. Noises around the house could also be heard, creaking of floor boards as if someone was again walking around.

I next heard the words "Mushrooms, they're really good for you", in my left ear! I really love mushrooms but also found out following this that humans have some sort of mushroom make up in their DNA! I suspect there is more to the mushroom than we currently realise!

Suddenly saw a nasty lizard looking eye. This made me jump initially and I knew that this was again not of love and light. I said more firmly this time to this being "If you are not of love and light, then go away". It went immediately. (This was possibly a tester to make sure I'd learned from the previous meditation)!

I was aware that I had had a conversation with someone but can't remember the content of the conversation, although I do seem to remember the name 'Paddy' being said (My Uncle).

Then had the image of a person (again, not sure who) put their hands on their knees, and lean towards me and gave me a kiss on the lips. This felt so real and I am convinced I had slipped into another reality momentarily. This gently disappeared and I had the vision of a beautiful baby, wrapped in white robes laughing and very happy. This in turn made me feel very happy. The vision began to fade leaving only the imprint of a smiling face. (This was very similar to a dream I had the night before).

I could then see the bottom of a pair of legs on my left hand side with bare feet, muscular legs and the tips of a set of wings curled around them. I next felt myself being led up a set of stairs surrounded by a kind of crystal mountain.

At one point during this meditation I could actually feel someone's hands on my head, as if conducting some kind of healing on me and my third eye chakra was being worked very hard!!

5. Our crystal was once again present.

I had a vision of an old black lady standing in the doorway of her home. She was smiling and waving goodbye as she was shutting the door. I imagined what she would do now following that, being on her own inside the house. Then saw myself with the lady in her house, hugging her and sending so much Love. I believe this followed on from meditation 1 where I was shown about old people being lonely and suffering.

I suddenly heard two or three times the words "Paul 7, Paul 7, Paul 7". I now think that 'Paul' is in fact Ascended Master Paul the Venetian and the '7' was a sign once again that I was on the right path.

I then saw an old wooden house in the middle of a wood. There was someone on the inside looking out but I don't know who. Next was the vision of a young polish lady, pregnant and wanting to go to school but was turned away because she was Polish. Heard the words "Just because she's not from here doesn't mean she can't go to Twickenham!! Twickenham was my old primary school and I think this was a message about not discriminating against anyone just because they are different to you.

A beautiful face suddenly appeared. It was that of a young male, round about in his 20's with pointed ears and short, curly, dark hair. He had a smile on his face like he was pleased to see me and seemed very proud. He gently disappeared.

I saw a small ball, sized like a ping pong which was fiery red/orange in colour with a morphing fiery effect going on inside of it. This ball was placed just within my left ear. Whilst I could see this I was actually feeling something going on with my left ear, a gentle and pleasant sensation. Again, this could have been some kind of healing.

I then found myself inside someone's living room with a youngish man and an old man sat on a sofa near to me. A voice shouted something about taking the dog out. The young man then said to the old man "You're not going out, you're staying here". It seemed as though the old man was being mistreated like a dog, not allowed his own say or freedoms and living by someone else's unfair rules.

The picture of an old man's feet wearing a pair of battered old sandals popped into my head. His feet were in bad shape with yellow and black toe nails. Not nice!

6. Crystal present.

Struggled to concentrate properly on this occasion but initially had the image of a beautiful lady and heard the name 'Suzie'. Then had the vision of someone going through a dilemma of some sort. I heard the words "And we almost always seem to be in one", meaning a dilemma.

An eagle appeared again looking straight towards me. This time the eagle was a golden eagle whereas before it had been a bald eagle (also known as the American eagle). This eagle then morphed into an owl with eyes still looking straight at me with little pointed ears.

I next saw colours swirling together, white, green and violet. First they were around me. Then I saw in front of me a blue male being, possibly Hindu. I could only see him from the torso up. He was swirling in the colours, waving at me with one hand and smiling. I believe this was Ascended Master Krishna who is a blue coloured deity.

Then I saw a white horse standing with his body facing to the right but with his head and neck looking down and to his left. This slowly faded away. Just before coming round I saw an Angel, I think male with his wings outstretched in an 'M' shape, smiling.

7. Angel class with crystal present.

We were guided to enter through into the crystal. I did this and saw myself in white garments on a white horse, peacefully cantering around.

I started to lose concentration for a moment and in that moment I heard the words "Concentrate, you can giggle about it later". Felt this was my Guardian Angel again keeping me in line as I could hear the class facilitator snoring having gone deep into the meditation! This tickled me.

I could feel Mick's Guardian Angel near and I saw a Native American chief wearing a feathered head piece. This faded out and I came out of the meditation.

8. Crystal present.

Both ears, especially my left were really ringing. Went in through crystal and put my hand into crystal hand print on wall. Saw myself again, in white robes, long flowing brown hair and again on a white horse. The horse turned into a unicorn.

I was aware of being in conversation with some people I believe were Ascended Masters although cannot recall who. They were giving me titles to books I needed to look at, all spiritual I believe but again I cannot recall any of the titles. I seemed to be in a big library, sliding around from one book to the next. This could possibly have been the Akashic library where the Akashic records are kept and is a term referring to a universal filing system which records every occurring thought, word, and action of human experience.

I suddenly had a great light shining in my eyes as if I was in a room filled with light. As I realised this it disappeared. I was aware of a large ball of white light and inside this was Ascended Master Jesus. I also kept hearing the name Paul being mentioned again but I can't remember why. I had called for the masters to be present so this could possibly have been Paul the Venetian again.

I remember the words "And we've all been there, and have been burned with fear", or something similar. Not sure what this was referring to. I had a vision of me with two Siberian Husky dogs in a basket, fully grown, both wolf grey. Was hugging them and interacting with them but it was as though I could actually feel them and their unconditional love for me. Then I saw the silhouette of a cat which disappeared almost immediately as it had appeared.

Before finishing the meditation I got the image of a pyramid made from gold with different pictures appearing on the front of it. The only one I can remember was of a white dove whose wings suddenly opened upwards and fully outstretched.

9. With clear quartz crystal.

I first began getting funny sensations in my right ear. Felt as though someone was reaching gently inside so much so I could feel my ear drum vibrating quickly causing it to tickle along with around my ear and down my neck. This continued for around 15 minutes. I kept saying "If you are of Love and Light then you can stay, if not then go away". This sensation continued each time. It felt like some kind of spiritual operation on my ear! Possibly opening it up?

I asked for my Guardian Angel to make contact with me and allow me to feel his wings. Each time I sensed a flash of light in front of my eyes which moved to the side as if a being of light was walking past. I had tingly sensations up and down my left arm and felt very warm as if wrapped up in his wings.

Next I had a vision of the Cottage Healing Centre and was aware of a voice speaking to me. The conversation was about doing spiritual talks in the future. The voice said to me "You are sometimes the nervous party but this will change in the future". I had picked an Angel card that day that was about workshops and seminars and maybe conducting them in the future!

An eagle appeared for a brief moment flying past with a fleeting glance in my direction.

I then asked the Angels if there was some kind of blockage in our new venture preventing it from working. I was aware of someone speaking to me about it but the only thing I can remember was the words "The skill, the skill", being repeated.

Heard lots of creaking upstairs and around me.

10. Ascended Master workshop.

Whilst in meditation about the Masters and after spending time with Mother Kwan Yin, we were asked to now call out for the Master who wanted to connect with us the most at that time. I immediately had the image of Paul the Venetian spring into mind. We had to hold that thought whilst pictures were being laid on the floor in the other room, face down. We all finished the meditation and then had to go and stand by a group of pictures that were drawing us to them. I was drawn to a group of four all face down in the top corner of the room. When they were turned over the Master for my group was Paul the Venetian!

11. Crystal present.

I did my usual protection calling in my Guardian Angel and Archangel Michael.

I set two goals for this meditation, the first being to find out the name of my Atlantean Guardian Angel. The second was to find out if I had a connection with Ashtar Command and if so to receive some sort of contact.

I drifted for a while but all of a sudden had the words "Dance 71" come into my head. This was shortly after extended to "Diana dance 71". I have no idea what this means if anything at all as yet. I also kept seeing the name 'Methuselah' but didn't feel this was the name of my Guardian. I was aware I had been drifting for quite a bit and so pulled myself back into line and said boldly in my head "I want to know the name of my Guardian Angel". Within a second the name "Corey" was written in my mind. I said "Thank you" and then enquired about Ashtar Command. I suddenly was aware that I was next to a massive mother ship, so big I could hardly see any of it as it was beyond my perimeter of vision. However, there was a contraption that seemed to be a part of the ship. It was a long downward dome shaped metallic object with the same underneath it leaving a gap between the two. The end was a beautiful glowing magenta colour and there were smaller objects popping out from here in a controlled motion, like smaller ships. I believe this was something to do with the Ashtar Command part of my request.

I was then in the back garden of my Dad's house at night on my own when I saw written in the sky in the same magenta colour, and also heard out loud the words "There's a fight coming". I immediately felt this was to do with the fight of good and bad. These words were then said: "But you shouldn't be afraid of it. There is nothing to be afraid of".

I then began to think of Mick and had this overwhelming love for him. I remember thinking "I Love Mick so much". This Love then extended toward our families and then out to everyone out in the world! It was a beautiful feeling and whilst I could feel it the meditation seemed to flow so much easier.

I then began to drift before coming out of the meditation.

12. During Reiki level two course.

I had images of myself on a wooden ship, high up and holding onto the wooden frames that hold the sails. It was stormy weather and there was someone facing me that said the words "Just start these little bits again from the last life".

This would appear to be a past life issue that needed to be addressed in this life and may have been holding me back in some way causing some kind of energetic blockage. Anything that is not properly addressed and dealt with in a past life, sometimes karmic, can be brought with you into the next life time and it will keep coming back until it has been addressed. This is where the Violet Flame comes in and it can be used to burn away and transmute these chords of old un-serving blockages and help us to move on with our lives.

Many of the messages in our meditations are yet to be understood. Some are quite serious in tone, some are downright funny and some completely obscure! Some of them still don't have any meaning to us at this point but we know that when it is relevant all shall be revealed to us. You don't have to be a guru to receive these messages. Just set yourself some quiet time and listen to the thoughts and feelings you experience. Your heart and intuition will guide you.

We are all capable and there is no one individual on this planet that these abilities aren't available to. Let's all use them and turn this place back into the paradise it was intended to be!

CHAPTER 12: CONCLUSION

Neither myself nor Sarah were spiritual people until the events covered in this book started happening to us and continue to happen to us, sometimes on a daily basis. We had never delved in to this subject or had any knowledge of it and I must say if I am being honest, never ever had any interest in it either. It was always the life style of the minority and this minority didn't include ourselves.

But you can't help but change your thinking and opinions when spiritualism finds you and finds you in a life changing way! When this happens to you, you have to sit up and take notice because everything that you once believed or were taught and told has to be re-evaluated. We were just 'Stuck in the Rut' people working and accepting what life had to throw at us, not realising that life was never meant to be limiting or stressful, It was meant to be exciting, happy, abundant and full of love for your fellow man and woman. But somehow we got it backwards and we all see the consequence of unfair systems of life everyday.

When you become spiritual you become free. Freedom is your right and no-one can interfere with that fact. We are so glad to have found our way on to this path, although it was in a shock to the system way for us. But if that shock had not have happened then we may have had a life time of a system that doesn't serve the vast majority who struggle every day to survive. How can this ever be justified?

You don't have to live under a regime of control. YOU ARE IN CONTROL. YOU ARE FREEDOM.

Society is stacked in the favour of those running it, not the people who are forced to live under the legislation and control imposed by those serving themselves. However things are changing and old systems are crumbling before our very eyes. One day soon society will be how it once was, fair and community spirited, where everyone's needs are met and the only rule is LOVE. We can't wait for that day but we must be at one and stand up for ourselves to hasten the process. We have lots of support in this goal from above but we have to build our own foundations. It is our planet. We live on her and we must take care of what is ours.

The universe is full of abundance and if we ask we get. It is the 'Law of Attraction'. God sees us all as his children no matter what your religion, race or background and he wants us all to have the very best of everything.

Would you want any less for your children?

Our journey although in time has been short, in knowledge and experience terms we are on an accelerated learning course. Sarah and I do not yet know where this journey is taking us but we have faith and confidence and it feels right. We have been called into spiritual service! It doesn't need a name, it just is what it is and it makes us happy. We are each our own temples.

Our hope is that the contents of this book will inspire you to see that there is another way and that there is hope for the future! If you experience any of the events that we have then you will know that you are not alone. It is reassuring to realise that there are always like minded people close to you. We were fortunate enough to have this help when we went through a frightening period in our lives. We found the Cottage Healing Centre, and within its walls were the answers to many of our questions.

You will never understand the world of spirit by looking through the eyes of human restraint. If you accept that everything is possible and allow your mind to be open and free, then it will be.

We know that our experiences will not end here and will continue to occur, but that's for another day, another time, and maybe even another book!

Keep fighting the good fight and make that light shine even more brightly!

In Love, Light and lots of Laugher,

GOD & GODDESS BLESS TO YOU ALL

NAMASTE!

Michael & Sarah